I0192392

The Horse in War

The Horse in War

Horses & Mules in the Allied Armies
During the First World War, 1914-18

D. S. Tamblyn

LEONAUR

The Horse in War
Horses & Mules in the Allied Armies
During the First World War, 1914-18
by D. S. Tamblyn

First published under the title
"The Horse in War"
and
Famous Canadian War Horses

Leonaur is an imprint of Oakpast Ltd

Copyright in this form © 2011 Oakpast Ltd

ISBN: 978-0-85706-785-2 (hardcover)
ISBN: 978-0-85706-786-9(softcover)

http://www.leonaur.com

Publisher's Notes

The views expressed in this book are not necessarily
those of the publisher.

Contents

Dedicated to the memory of the
Late Major-General J. L. Lipsett, C.B., C.M.G., D.S.O
The Soul of the 3rd Canadian Division

Preface

In this book it is intended to depict to the reader, with as few words as possible, the part played by the horse in the Great War, and this I trust has been accomplished with the aid of the illustrations contained therein. The intention is to place any profits derived from the sale of this book (as at time of first publication), into the hands of the Kiwanis Club—for use in connection with their work of the under-privileged child—and the Society for the Prevention of Cruelty to Animals in their work of assisting those who cannot speak for themselves.

My many thanks are extended to General Sir Arthur Currie for his foreword and appreciation.

Mr. H. G. Waites, of Toronto, the noted animal artist, for his assistance in reproducing the majority of the famous Canadian horses which have added greatly to the attraction of the book.

I am also grateful to the R. S. P. C. A., London, England, for permission to reproduce a number of their pictures.

To the publishers of the *Tatler* and *Sphere* of London, England, for their kind permission to reproduce the picture entitled "Good Bye, Old Man"; they own the copyright, and are prepared to supply photogravure and coloured copies.

To the *Cavalry Journal* for their kind permission to reproduce the picture entitled "Lance versus Lance."

To Messrs. Tugwell and Company, of Toronto, for a number of Canadian Official Photographs.

I also wish to express my appreciation to Mrs. T. Girling, of Victoria, B.C., for permitting me to print the late Captain T.

Girling's poem entitled *Dumb Heroes*, which was written under shell fire by that officer while serving with me in the Third Canadian Division.

The little book entitled *The Salient and Other Poems* written by the late Captain T. Girling is an outstanding feature in poetical works and should appeal to all lovers of horses.

Captain T. Girling's untimely death was directly due to his untiring attentions to his dumb friends on the field of battle.

To Canon F. G. Scott, C.M.G., D.S.O., and Lt.-Colonel A, F. Duguid, D.S.O., for their assistance.

Foreword

War, we are told, brings out and develops all the worst in the character of men.—cruelty, callousness, the lust to kill. The statement would be truer were it not one-sided, for who can forget the example of untarnishable honour and flaming valour which shone amid the horror and the darkness of strife? Who can forget the deeds of kindliness and self-sacrifice which proved that the soul of man still held the divine spark.

Alleviating influences there always were, even through the bitterest days of combat, even through the long, drab days and nights in rain-sodden camp or mud-filled trench and among the few bright things of the soldier's life none touched him more deeply than the mutual attachment of man and horse.

No one who has ever had to do with soldiers and with horses can fail to acknowledge how much the horse helped to keep up the morale of the man. The very work of tending a horse was a distraction which relieved the trooper or the gunner from the otherwise unrelenting tension of warfare. The few minutes of pleasant companionship made him the more ready for the battle of a new day.

There are others than those who shared in it who know how real was this alliance; there are others than the drivers and the riders who appreciate how essential was the horse to the efficiency of our fighting machine.

The horse could neither speak for himself nor help himself, patient and ready to do his work in the misery of rain and slime, under the sudden pain of wounds looked to the man for every-

THE FAMOUS EQUINE STATUE, CALGARY, ALBERTA

thing, and the man, as well as he could, provided the need. The gunner on a long march walked to save his horse, and at the end of it, weary though he was, gave the more weary beast such comfort as he might, before taking thought for himself.

Well indeed did the horse repay any care that was expended upon him. Hauling transport waggons far beyond the point which mechanical transport could reach and over roads they could not travel, dragging guns on long cross country routes, carrying troopers to a fight and messengers to a signal station, he played a splendid and an essential role in every operation of war.

Alexander and Bucephalus, Napoleon and his white charger may perhaps fill a greater space on the page of history than the driver and the horse of the battery of field artillery or the trooper and the steed of the regiments of lancers and hussars, yet one partnership was no more important or significant than the other; every man and charger of the Canadian Cavalry Brigade riding across the bullet-swept valley of Cayeux in the Battle of Amiens, every trooper and steed of the deathless six hundred of the Crimea have a place together on the page of glory.

Colonel Tamblyn in this book written with so much care and skill has shown not only the knowledge of horses which we who served with him learned to expect of him, but a high appreciation of the services rendered by the old-age partnership of horse and man and a real love for the dumb friends who served their masters so bravely and so well.

A. W. Currie.

CHAPTER 1

Remounts

Very little has been recorded regarding "The Horse in War," so in this short account it is intended to relate how man's co-partner, the horse, fared and suffered in the late war.

The majority of people are surprised when they learn that at the end of 1918, Great Britain had over one million horses and mules in the different theatres of war. As can be imagined, this entailed a great deal of worry for those responsible for the care of these animals.

Let us consider our dumb friends from the time they left their homes, be it in the city, the rural districts, or the western prairies of the Dominion of Canada. Many thousands came from the wide open spaces where peace and quiet are undisturbed and where the sons of men are few and far between. Can you imagine the appalling change from the quiet of the open spaces to the shambles that existed in France and Flanders.

Regardless of the place from which they came, all were accorded the same treatment upon being taken over by the army officials. The collecting and selecting of this unprecedented conscription of "horse power" was undertaken by the Remount Department. The undertaking was of tremendous proportions and called for the employment of representatives in every corner of the globe.

If ever there was a real conscription of "The Fit" it was applied in the case of the horse and the mule. They came in thousands from England, Ireland, Scotland, Canada, the United States of America, Australia, The Argentine Republic, and so on, *ad lib*. India furnished a small mule suitable for pack purposes, and the Argentine sent a larger and stronger mule, which was used chiefly for draft duties.

The officers representing the Remount Department were charged with selecting the types required; that is to say, they had to decide whether the animals were suitable for "Light Draft," "Heavy Draft," "Tack" or "Riding." All these types were required for the various branches of the service. The heavy draft were used for the transportation of heavy guns and supplies; the light draft for field guns, 18 pounders; and 4.5 howitzers; pack animals for packing guns and ammunition over the little-known trails and roads of the mountainous countries in the eastern theatre of war and into what was known as the "forward areas" in France and Flanders. The riding horses were used chiefly by the cavalry and mounted infantry in the eastern theatre of war, Asia, Palestine, and Mesopotamia.

Upon completion of the classification, all animals were subjected to veterinary examination to determine their physical soundness and to ascertain whether or not they were free from contagious and infectious diseases. Those found free from disease and physically fit were accepted.

From this stage of initiation the lot of these animals was not a happy one. They were officially taken over by the Remount Officers, taught how to behave, to respond to the orders of the rein, just as a soldier is taught to respect the "Order of Command." In many instances horses and mules objected to this intensive training, possibly figuring that they should not be called upon to do any work, or to fit themselves for the difficult and hard times ahead.

Is the horse endowed with powers of reason? From my experience in handling and caring for this animal, I conclude that he is. Time after time I have seen him reject new ideas, when an attempt was made to thrust them upon him, and yet, when he was educated to what was wanted of him, he would go plodding along, doing his duty, in a manner that was an example to all.

REMOUNT IN BREAKING
The Author's Horse (Drawn from life)

The mule, too, gives one food for thought. He can, at times, be a most disagreeable fellow; on the other hand, when conditions seem to meet with his ideas of what is right, and what is coming to him, he is faithful and willing.

However, to continue, once the animals have been broken to understand thoroughly just what is expected of them, they are classed as having been trained sufficiently to permit being sent to the different units of the army; in other words, their recruit stage has been completed and the animals take their places beside the "seasoned warriors."

In the case of horses and mules from foreign parts, they were shipped across the high seas in horse transports especially fitted for their comfort. Usually six hundred to eight hundred animals were shipped in each transport, and all horse transports carried a veterinary officer and ample veterinary supplies to attend their medical wants; also, each animal had a separate stall.

Animals on the upper deck of the boats were provided with rugs, but those on the lower decks were not. The lower decks were supplied with fresh air, which was sent down by canvas wind sails with a wide bell mouth, arranged from the rigging, while electric fans drove out the foul air. By these means the lower decks were kept ventilated, thereby permitting the animals to travel in comfort in this respect. Ample food and fresh water was supplied in all ships. Further, the animals were exercised daily and their stalls kept clean.

The navy rendered noble services by convoying the horse transports from the country of their origin to the war-ridden countries of France and Flanders.

The journey on water was fraught with danger. The submarine when it was least expected, laid in wait and often caught the animals like rats in a trap. There was no possible chance of saving them; to see these animals drown and to be utterly powerless to render aid was a terrible sight for those in charge of the transport.

This was the first thrilling stage of the career of the horse in war; for when a ship was torpedoed he seemed to have a prescience and by neighing and a restless demeanour in the stalls, he would give warning of the approach of danger.

It is a well-known fact that the hunnish instinct of the German submarine commanders caused them to have pictures taken of these ghastly scenes, which were exhibited in Germany during the war. This will go down, very far down into history as one of their hellish atrocities.

It was here that our dumb friends entered what can be properly called the second stage of their adventurous career. Once landed in Europe, the remounts were rushed to depots, and from there to divisions to be further distributed among brigades, where they were again distributed among the respective units of the brigade. Here they took their place beside the seasoned warriors and were almost immediately put into harness or under saddle. Like men, they often penetrated the forward areas the night following their arrival at the brigade; many failed to return to their new home, having sacrificed their lives in order that our men should not want for supplies or ammunition; those that returned carried on day in and day out.

The transportation duties were heavy. The heavy horse transports were responsible for the transportation of rations and supplies from the divisional rail-head to the divisional dumps, where the unit transports proceeded daily for their supplies of rations, and returned with them to their own transport lines, at which points the rations were divided and distributed to the companies.

In event of a unit being in the front line, the unit's transport work was doubled by the fact that not only did the supplies have to be brought to their transport lines and divided, but it was also necessary for the supplies to be taken into the vicinity of the front line trenches. To carry this into effect the horses and mules were constantly under fire of the heavy and the light field artillery of the enemy, as well as machine gun and rifle fire in some instances. Exposed as were these animals, without cover, save only darkness, they accomplished their task with a feeling that a duty done was a victory won.

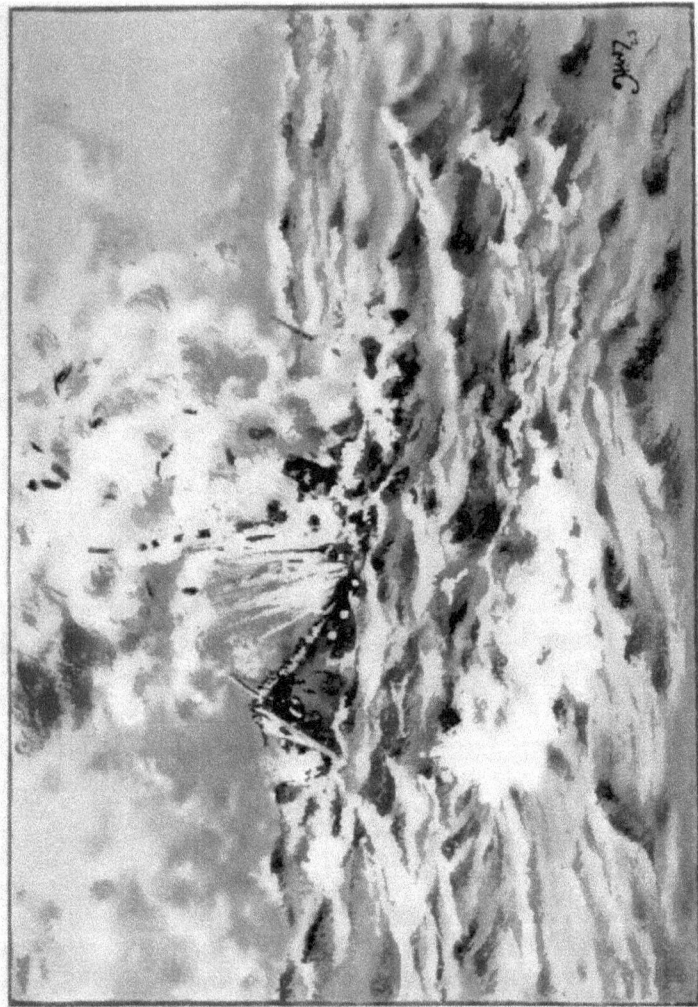

HORSE TRANSPORT

Submarine attack on a Horse Transport, with fatal results.

I remember one very outstanding case of a supply cart horse belonging to one of the Canadian artillery units. After the horse and his rider had delivered the supplies to a party of men in advance of Spree Farm, near Ypres, this horse and its driver proceeded homeward to the horse lines, a field about one and a half miles from Vlamertinghe (East). Passing through St. Jean and Ypres, they continued past what was known as the asylum, where a shell exploded close by, killing the driver in the cart, and mortally wounding the horse.

This did not mar the sagacity of the horse, for it continued down the Vlamertinghe Road to the railway crossing, where it turned first left, then sharp left again, and continued down a side road for nearly one mile, whence it turned left into a field where its lines were, and stopped. The picket on duty went to give assistance to unhitch the horse, and to his surprise found the master dead in the waggon from shell wounds. Examining the horse, he found its entrails trailing on the ground, and before he could unhitch the poor animal it dropped dead. Like its master it had made the supreme sacrifice and added one more hero to the list of dumb animals who cannot speak for themselves. This was but one of the many horses that gave their lives.

Apart from transportation of supplies, the artillery horses and mules rendered service not to be forgotten. Each packing eight shells to the load, in rain and sleet, with mud to their hips and shoulders, over planked, fascine, and unbroken roads, over shell holes and bog, these animals supplied ammunition to the gun pits, led forward by a solitary man, with but one thought—victory.

At night this was both a pitiful and thrilling sight. Under cover of darkness, the explosion of shells and Verey lights in the distance, the aeroplanes overhead bombing indiscriminately, the occasional sound of gas alarms, the neighing of horses and mules, made the tension almost unbearable; yet our dumb friends continued night after night, apparently realizing, I feel sure, that ammunition was essential to those in the front.

The question of "who won the war" has oft-times been asked.

To my mind there is only one reply; man and his co-partners, the horse and the mule, for without the horse the war would have been lost, and, as an old friend of mine once stated, "Germany in my opinion had no chance of winning a protracted war, because she had no resources in horses, and the fact that the Allies had command of the seas and of the horse population of the world was a weapon in their hands which went a long way towards the downfall of the enemy. No one knew that better than Germany.

To depict the hardships that artillery horses endured, I feel the pictures herein suffice, for the centre-piece of this book is the greatest touch of human nature one could wish to witness, and I have actually seen many such sights. The words "Goodbye, Old Man" and the expression of the horse itself, seemingly knowing just what his master is saying, appeals to anyone looking at the picture.

PACK ANIMALS
Packing Ammunition into Ypres Salient. Note mud condition.

HORSE STANDINGS
Somewhere in Flanders

CHAPTER 2

Care and Management of the Horse in War

We have seen in the foregoing-pages how the horse and the mule suffered in war. Now let us look at their life from another aspect, care and management of such animals in war, and their wants from a veterinary point of view.

From the sketches of the stables, you will note that horses and mules were protected from wind and rain, and where traverses were provided, from bomb and shell splinters. This protection was very necessary, because it was most essential to keep horses and mules physically fit, in order that they might carry out their various duties. Horses exposed to adverse conditions soon became debilitated, and if this were permitted the animals would fail in their task to deliver the rations and the ammunition to those in the forward areas dependent upon them, and would in many instances through their physical weakness fall by the wayside.

Although the provision of traverses protected animals from bomb and shell splinters, and not from any direct hit of such missiles, it was surprising how many lives were saved by bringing these traverses into effect. No time was lost by transport officers, when moving from one area to another, in providing protection for their animals. Of course, during an offensive operation this was not always possible, and consequently our animal casualties were greatly increased. However, traverses were provided whenever possible, for men loved their horses and mules, and risked their lives countless times for their protection.

To a certain extent equine dugouts were used. The object of these dugouts was similar to that of providing stables with traverses, but they were constructed more particularly for the purpose of deceiving the enemy aircraft. Such dugouts were camouflaged with tufts of grass which made it impossible for the aviators to locate them. By this means horses and mules were given much more protection than if exposed in stables or open lines.

There were times when it was found necessary to concentrate troops for attack, and under these conditions horses and mules were picketed in open fields. This was done during the battles of Vimy, Passchendaele and the Somme. On these occasions only earthworks were thrown around lines; they worked well in dry weather, but the rainy season sometimes prevented such protection being formed. Nothing more distressing could be witnessed than a concentration of transport animals, during wet seasons, in fields where the mud was over their knees and hocks. Horses were wet and cold for months at a time; grooming was out of the question, and where overhead hay-net lines were not brought into use, the hay was trampled into the mud. Under these conditions debilitated horses, which were propped up by the mud, died on their feet. Men lay day after day in their wet clothing beside the lines of their dumb friends, equally sharing their lot.

The men did what they could under the circumstances to provide for their charges. Warm feed and chaffed hay, carrots and linseed were given to them when possible, but even these at times did not satisfy the ravenous appetites of the horses and mules. They would grab the blankets of their mates and devour portions of them, while to witness mules choking in the endeavour to eat their hay-nets was fairly common. On more than one occasion I have seen them grab the epaulets from men's shoulders, ravenous for the want of food. Why this condition you may ask? It was due to the lack of bulk food brought about

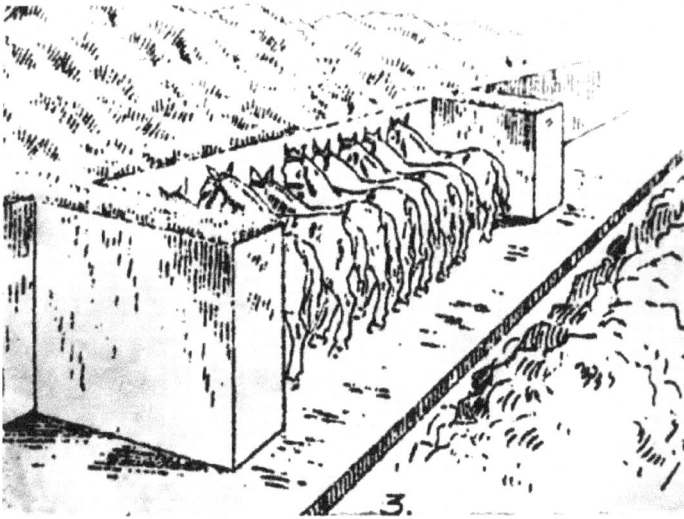

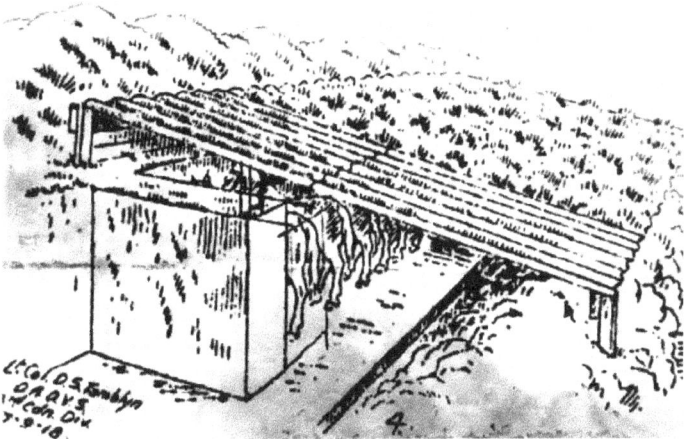

THE TAMBLYN EQUINE DUGOUT
Note the Camouflage from Aeroplane Attack.

by the animals not being able to partake of it, under the conditions that existed. For instance, horses fed from hay-nets tied to breast-ropes, trampled from fifty *per cent*, to seventy *per cent*, of their hay into the mud; twenty *per cent*, of their oats and other rations were tossed from their nose bags. This, together with the extreme exposure, soon left them in a very debilitated condition, and having reached such a state, they became deplorable in the extreme.

Many schemes were improvised to overcome the uncomfortable conditions which our horses contended with. Wind screens were made from burlap stretched from post to post; boilers for heating food were made by men in the field from sheets of galvanized iron. This made it possible to give the horses and mules warm food at night and also in the daytime when the weather was wet and cold.

Overhead hay-net lines were also brought into use. This means of suspending hay-nets led to a great saving of hay, and thereby kept the horses and mules much more contented because they received the bulk food which was so very essential during the tedious periods of hard work and adverse climatic conditions.

To ensure the supply of water in itself constituted a great task which was carried out efficiently by the Engineer Corps. Troughs had to be provided in most instances, to which water was conveyed in pipes.

At the battle of Vimy, water was obtainable on the high peak of the ridge the day following the battle. I always considered this one of the best pieces of work of laying water pipes ever witnessed in France. It was a very pleasant sight to see man, horses and mules in a position to get water so far from a source of supply, and I am sure they appreciated it.

At most water troughs it was necessary to provide a time schedule to prevent congestion around the troughs and to permit all units to water their animals. This system obtained the very best of results. When watering from ponds or rivers, it was necessary to prevent disturbing the water, and to enable this to be effected pails or pumps with hose connections, which extended into the middle of the pond, were used. Under no circumstances were the animals led into the pond, nor were men permitted to wash in the pond or its vicinity, for the least suspicion of the presence of soap would cause horses to refuse to drink, as they were very particular what they ate or drank.

During the winter months heavy rugs were provided for the horses and mules. These afforded them much comfort, but owing to the continuous tearing of the same by animals in a playful mood, the life of the new rug in some instances was only that of a few days.

During dry weather and with animals under cover, grooming was carried out with regularity, as if under peace conditions. This was very essential as a preventive measure against skin diseases, which became prevalent during the winter months, while it also permitted the removal of mud, and the drying of their limbs, which went a long way towards keeping them warm.

The shoeing of horses and mules required very close supervision, and faulty shoeing was remedied without fail.

I remember when our horses and mules, traversing the fascine roads at Passchendaele, wrenched the shoes from their feet owing to the fault of shoeing animals long at the heels. At one particular period our animals were returning without a shoe on their feet at all, consequently increasing our casualties to an alarming extent.

This, however, was remedied by shoeing short at the heels; in fact the divisional order which was sent out required all horses and mules that were being used on that particular work to be shod with practically no heel at all to the shoe. Farriers worked incessantly under adverse conditions, watching the individual animals, with a view to remedying any fault in shoeing. Their work was not always appreciated by the commanding officers owing to their inability to understand the effects, but those who were horsemen and interested themselves in the detailed care of their animals, always consulted their farriers and exhibited a great interest; so much so, that in some brigaded shoeing com-

YPRES

Transport hurrying through the town to escape the fate of those animals beside the debris

petitions were arranged quite often and prizes were given to the farriers for the best shod unit and for individual animals. This all stimulated the work of the farriers and tended to promote efficiency in this art.

The care of our animals' feet was all-important from an army point of view, for, as Lt.-General Sir A. C. Macdonell once mentioned to me: "No shoe, no foot; no foot, no horse; no horse, no transport; no transport, no battalion!"

It will be observed, then, that the efficiency of the farriery staff was all-important to any mounted unit.

BOMBS

Time Bombs—From the point of view of animal protection there were several types of bombs to contend with; those laid by the enemy as traps for the advancing troops were known as time and concussion bombs. They were usually laid beneath the floor of the stables, either in the stall or directly under the floor, at the entrance. These timed bombs would explode, if not detected, just when everyone had settled for the night, and, detonating with an upward force, would play havoc with the animals within the stables.

Concussion Bombs—These exploded upon contact, which is caused usually by the impact of the feet of the horse directly over them, and if a number of horses were in the immediate vicinity, the casualties would be large. I am very much pleased to state, however, that this inhuman machine did not work out very often against the Canadian troops, for prior to the occupation of any stables, the premises were thoroughly inspected by the men of the Engineer Corps or else by the transport officer himself—another instance of men risking their lives to protect their dumb charges.

Torpedo Bombs—Torpedo bombs dropped from low-flying planes came into play. One particular instance, I remember well at Ouderdum over our transport lines; a number of bombs were dropped, one of which went through the roof, clean through the horse standing directly beneath, killing the horse instan-

31

taneously and bursting upon the floor below, but luckily only wounding two other horses.

The Razor Bomb—The razor bomb appeared the most dangerous, especially in open lines, where no protection had been provided. These bombs were so constructed that they exploded about a foot above the ground, with the result that the bomb splinters would strike the legs and abdomen of our horses; in fact, in many instances our animals were completely disembowelled.

I have already mentioned the preventive measures taken against bombs, and where such measures were adopted, the casualties were very much lighter than where no protection was given the animals.

PACK ANIMALS
Packing ammunition into the gun pits at Ypres salient.

CHAPTER 3

Battles

Ypres—Ypres salient, which was held so long by the Canadians, was a dismal spot, while the town itself as time went on was nothing more than a heap of debris which bore evidence to the amount of shelling. During the many months the Canadians held the salient against German aggression, transports had to pass through to supply those in the front line, dependent upon the horse and mule for supplies and ammunition.

The movements of transports through Ypres was a slow process. There were two roads, the Poperinghe Road and the Ouderdon Road. The former was always congested, but thanks to the Road Controls, we were able to regulate the traffic, so as to enable a few wagons to go ahead at one time, and thus reduce the number of casualties in breaking through the shelled areas.

Verey lights of different colours were seen popping up from the trenches, illuminating the whole area around, so much so that the silhouette of men, horses and wagons could be seen on the high ground around Ypres, especially in the vicinity of China Wall, where transports came under machine gun fire as well as artillery. Transports, making their way to their respective units' headquarters, which would be situated at some remote spot such as Ration Farm, Maple Copse, Zillebeke, being the town of Zellebeke itself, or the famous ramparts which formed part of the defence of Ypres and which provided absolute shell-proof cover for the brigade and other headquarters, were always met at the entrance to Ypres on the eastern side.

At these points ration parties met the transports and carried their rations to their respective units, and the transports, under cover of darkness, then took to their heels, and by continuing on the road directly in the rear of the front line trenches, returned to their horse lines.

Transportation work was carried on at night as much as possible, for obvious reasons, the most important being for the purpose of avoiding observation by aeroplanes, observation balloons and artillery O.P.'s, for immediately a transport was observed moving in the area by any of these means of observation, it would invariably come under the shell fire of the enemy, which often led to serious results.

Passchendaele—Passchendaele was certainly one of the most trying battles in which our horses and mules took part. The terrain over which they travelled can only be described as a quagmire. The earth was so disturbed with shell fire that its appearance was that of a sponge. The rains added to the difficulty of traversing it, so much so that practically at every step they would sink to their knees in liquid mud. Horses became mired to such an extent that it was a case of being humane to destroy them, for it was impossible to extricate any horse without risking three or more, and rather than leave horses and mules in such a predicament, they were destroyed, thus preventing them from becoming wounded through shell fire, and lying in agony for hours.

To lessen such occurrences, however, everything possible was done by the Engineer Branch of the Service. Plank and fascine roads were constructed forward of the divisional dumps, which made it possible for horses and mules to reach the gun pits and infantry advanced headquarters with a minimum amount of risk; but even with all these precautionary measures it was found necessary to pack in ammunition and supplies by pack animals.

The Battle of Passchendaele Ridge was one of the terrible experiences of the Great War for our dumb friends. The return of pack animals and their leaders from the forward areas was a sight never to be forgotten. Horses and men, plastered with mud

GUNS GOING INTO ACTION AT YPRES
Note condition of ground.

from head to foot, some exhibiting evidence of having received first aid treatment, others bearing ghastly wounds, and the carcasses of dead animals being used as stepping stones by the men to bring their charges and themselves out of the mire to more solid ground, made an awful picture.

Shrapnel and bombs were bursting here, there and everywhere; horses neighing, and men bidding the last farewell to their dumb pals, who probably had been their chums since the commencement of the war, made matters worse and more unbearable. Such sights cannot but be indelibly impressed on one's mind, and they will carry down in history the gallant deeds of our men, their horses and their mules.

Vimy Battle. Date April 9, 1917—I look upon the Battle of Vimy as Canada's Glorious Day, where her sons won everlasting fame, never to be forgotten. It was like a cub jumping to the assistance of its wounded dam.

The operations here were somewhat different. We had disturbed ground conditions, but these were not so bad as at Passchendaele in so far as the swampy conditions were concerned. The ground around Vimy had considerable amount of drainage, which Passchendaele did not have.

The concentration of every arm of the Service drawn by horses and mules was made directly in the rear of the Ridge. It was difficult to find space to park even the smallest transport units. Troops rehearsing the attack over tapes; engineer supplies and ammunition going forward for days prior to the attack; animals working to the uttermost limit; all in preparation for Canada's Day, was a sight for the gods.

Zero Hour—It seemed as if the bowels of the earth had developed into volcanic eruption and every available man and animal had been brought into the Service. Infantry went forward relentlessly, not knowing what the next hour would bring to them—death or victory. Our guns moved forward into their new positions continuously in leap-frog manner, until the village of Vimy was in our hands. Over mine craters and shell holes, the advance was a rough one. Ammunition was pushed forward in support of the guns. Engineering supplies followed our men in close order. Wounded men were evacuated by stretchers from the forward areas and by ambulance from the advanced dressing stations. Horses and mules returning showed evidence of having been wounded, some mortally, others slightly. Veterinary mobile sections worked to their limit collecting the more serious cases by ambulance and evacuating their patients to base hospitals, while, like our men, many dumb friends paid the price of victory with their lives, a triumph never to be forgotten by those who survived.

While Lord Byng knew within his own heart that he had behind him regiments that sized up to those of Wellington, a solid wall, there is no doubt he realized that to carry the battle to a successful conclusion it depended not only on men alone, but a great deal on horses and mules.

General Byng congratulated the officers and men of the different Canadian divisions that took part in the battle, and complimented the transport and veterinary services on their work of co-operation.

"Gases."

Gas was experienced at Vimy and Ypres, and many casualties occurred amongst our horses, but upon the cases being returned to a place known as Berthenwall Farm, all recovered under the care and treatment of our able Veterinary Staff.

We had to contend chiefly with two kinds of gas, chlorine and mustard. The former was sent over in cloud form and in shells, the latter in shells only. For the cloud gas we were warned from the front line by telephone, so that those in the rear transport lines could prepare for eventualities. Those men and animals caught in the immediate vicinity of the direct forward areas took to the high ground, other transports in ruins of towns made hurried exit, as the latter held gas clouds for long periods.

The use of horse gas masks was not practical, more especially under shell fire. Men were instructed to adjust their own masks and bring their animals to safety at a slow trot. Such advice was

SUICIDE CORNER (MIRAUMONT)
Depicting the road conditions over which
our animals were forced to travel.

responsible for the saving of the lives of many men and animals, because, prior to these instructions being issued, a great number of men and animals were killed and wounded in the attempt to adjust gas masks on animals during a gas attack.

Mustard gas was sent over chiefly by shells of long range guns, whose fire would be directed by enemy aircraft on to our transport lines.

Directly this was observed, the animals were cut loose and driven from the shelled areas, and when Fritz had decided he had done all the damage that could be done, the shelling would cease. The animals would then be returned to their lines, providing, of course, no shells had dropped within the actual lines, as contact with the ground where a mustard gas shell had exploded would be serious for any animal. The least touch of mustard gas on the body of an animal would produce a blister, which, when severe, led to sloughing of the skin.

Amiens—Great secrecy covered the Canadian entry into this great offensive, and never did Canadians fight with more courage. This was recognized by the French commander on our right, for in recognition thereof he decorated seventy-five Canadians with the *Croix de Guerre*. The Germans realized that they were opposed to a corps that knew not the meaning of the word "Surrender."

I often thought of the saying of an old lady in London, who upon seeing a number of our men passing by and noticing the word "Canada" on their shoulder straps, shouted after them, "Canadians, eh, never lost a trench." Great words to fall upon one's ears, and they sent a thrill of appreciation through one's own body.

The battle, from the time we entered it until we pulled out, was full of incidents. Never was there a battle so thrilling, never did so many arms of the service take part as on this occasion. Aeroplanes in combat, heavy and light artillery in action, cavalry and tanks charging across the country, infantry advancing and machine guns everywhere possible, routed the enemy at all points.

It was a modern battle, and one in which the horse and the mule played an inestimable part. One saw the light guns going forward taking up fresh positions and the cavalry cutting out from behind the cover of woods and ravines to take some new objective for the purpose of dislodging the enemy's machine guns and infantry. Strings of wounded men, horses and mules, with bandaged limbs, could also be seen staggering to the rear. Mobile veterinary sections could be detected busy in some remote corner of a field or garden, attending to the wounded and shipping the serious cases back to the evacuating station by road in Indian file or in ambulances.

There were many and varied scenes; tanks and horses *hors de combat;* the mad, desperate rush of ammunition to the forward areas; and men making every possible effort to take and hold the contested ground. It was a battle of movement, not as in other previous encounters, a condition of "Stalemate"; all were on tiptoe, with but one thought, to keep the enemy on the move and in the direction which we had all so long hoped he would take.

The bombing in this battle was terrible; in fact, I do not remember any other battle in which it was so severe. On the evening of August the tenth, our Third Section—Divisional Ammunition Column—was slightly to the right of the advance of Beaucourt, just off Roye Road. From the enemies' bombing planes this section came in for very severe casualties, which amounted to nearly eighty *per cent*, of their animals. Number One Company of the Thirty-second Divisional Train—British—immediately beside this section, suffered horse casualties equally as bad, if not worse. In this connection I wish to mention that the fright exhibited by the horses and mules was very marked. Bombing had started just at dusk, and continued throughout the night.

It appeared to me that directly bombing started, the horses and mules, by their constant unrest and continued neighing, realized that danger was near them. When bombs fell within the lines and horses and mules lay dead or mortally wounded, those

MULES TAKING SHELLS TO THE FIRING LINES IN SPECIALLY MADE PANNIERS

untouched realized the situation. To alleviate the situation, men ran to the sides of their animals, speaking words of encouragement, patting them and heading them away from the terrible scenes.

The following narrative by Captain L. E. L. Taylor, M.C.. records the keen instinct of a mule during the bombing above referred to:

While at Beaucourt. of 'happy memory,' after a particularly warm night, during which Number One Company, Thirty-second Divisional Train, lost over ninety *per cent*, of their animals, and Number Three Company, Canadian Divisional Ammunition Column—Captain Kruger, M.C.— at least eighty *per cent*, of theirs, one of my men found a badly wounded mule standing inside all that remained of a house, the animal being located in a more or less dark corner. Upon being notified, I went over to the place in question, and after examination, decided to destroy the poor beast. I instructed a non-commissioned officer to assist in bringing the animal into a field some forty or fifty feet distant.

Just as the men arrived with their charge at the place selected, a bomb dropped in the immediate neighbourhood, and directly afterwards, a sudden *rat, tat, tat* was heard overhead. Naturally, all eyes peered skywards and we were able to discern quite distinctly two German bombing planes hotly pursued by one of our air squadrons. No sooner did the noise to which I have referred commence than the mule broke away from the man who was holding him and started off, at a miserable crippled gait, for the old, shell-shattered building from which he had been taken. I found him in exactly the same position and trembling in every limb.

It was quite evident to me that this poor dumb beast had sought safety from the bombs, one of which had undoubtedly been the cause of its painful and fatal injuries, behind the walls which I have mentioned, for we experienced considerable difficulty in coaxing the animal out of its retreat a second time.

For protection against bombs there were many schemes. Unfortunately on this particular occasion our section only arrived at their new lines a few minutes before they were bombed, and it was very likely they were observed from the aeroplanes.

As a protection against bombs the most effective system was the equine dugout used in trench warfare, although the squaring of shell holes in open warfare gave good protection against bomb splinters. Traverses in the shape of Irish turf banks were also used with great success. Horses and men were bombed continually, yet when afforded protection such as that mentioned above, they escaped marvellously.

The careful selection of horse lines, under cover from observation and the placing of animals in groups, minimized the casualties to a great extent.

The question is often asked me, "Do horses and mules fear shelling?" My experience has been that horses do not fear shelling as much as bombing. They certainly realized the danger they were exposed to whenever enemy aviators started to bomb, and some were apparently able to recognize the difference between enemy aircraft and that of our own.

The following description by Captain L. E. L. Taylor, M.C., bears out this statement:

> While at Bruay, a black polo pony mare was admitted to the mobile veterinary section as suffering from shoulder lameness. This animal repeatedly gave warning of the approach of enemy aircraft in the following manner: She would stop eating, throw up her head, with ears erect, and stand perfectly still for a few moments in a listening attitude, then she would commence to neigh, stamp, paw, and act generally in an excited manner. A very few moments after these symptoms had been shown, enemy aircraft would be heard approaching, yet strange to say, this animal would continue to feed in an ordinary manner

GAS MASKS FOR THE HORSE AND MAN

should the noise which she heard—long before the men did—arise from our own bombing planes.

I have repeatedly stood and watched this animal's actions at night time, and came to the conclusion that she could distinguish the difference between the sound of our aircraft engines and that of the enemy, and connected the latter with a terrific detonation. As a result each time she heard a German plane she became very uneasy, if not actually panicky.

Cambrai—Prior to the Battle of Cambrai we were in rest at a place called Queant. I remember our Divisional Headquarters were situated in a quarry, and I thought the dugout entrance around the sides made an ideal form of protection. This fact, I feel sure, Corps Headquarters envied, for they were situated to the west of us, and were afforded little or no cover. While here, we laid to rest Major-General J. L. Lipsett, C.B., C.M.G., D.S.O., who, having been transferred from the Third Canadian Division to the Fourth British Division, was killed while surveying the country ahead of his men. He was a great lover of animals, a keen sportsman, a true solider, and he was beloved by all without exception; in short, he was the soul of the Third Division.

Our fight for Cambrai was a difficult one, and Bourlon Woods railway embankment immediately in front of the town stands out in one's mind. The exposure to aeroplane attacks and continuous bombing, day and night, gave all a feeling of uneasiness, and even our horses showed signs of terror by neighing and watchfulness.

One particular incident of comradeship that will always remain in my memory was exhibited during a night just prior to our entry into Cambrai. While advising a certain number of men to square shell holes so as to protect their animals, I came across a Canadian bugler boy who was assisting to throw up the earth around some transport horses, with a view to protecting them against bomb and shell splinters. Having done this, the lad dug a hole in the side of the road for his own protection.

At daybreak the following morning I happened to pass the

same spot and found that a bomb had dropped in the immediate vicinity of this little chap's cover, with the result that it loosened the earth with tragic consequences, while the horses he had helped to protect escaped injury, due in a great measure to his manly labour the previous night. It seemed to me that this lad's first thoughts were for the horses, a spirit which is bred in men who love animals.

While the fight was continuing at Cambrai, our troops pushed forward with all power possible. Artillery moved in the open, engineering material hastened forward for the construction of bridges over the canal just on the outskirts of the town. It was a sight; transports everywhere, artillery leap-frogging into new positions, infantry and machine gunners fighting their way and beating the Germans back foot by foot. Into the burning city our troops fought their way, to be confronted again with the hellishness of German culture—bombs, incendiary and explosive, timed and otherwise, letting forth their inferno and increasing within the hearts of our men a hate that can never die. Walls of houses falling into the streets, roofs collapsing, old men and women coming forth from their homes broken in heart and spirit, to meet their deliverers, many of whom had given their lives to rescue them, added to the horror.

Horse and mule transports pushed their way into the city of flames and collapsing walls. Mobile veterinary sections busied themselves evacuating those animals wounded in the attempt to push forward, and the carcasses of those animals that died lay along the route to the city inferno.

The evacuating of wounded animals from this battle was a tedious undertaking, owing to the distances between the forward troops, mobile veterinary sections and rail-head. However, no stones were left unturned to expedite this work with a view to alleviating the pain of our dumb friends.

Mons, 11 a.m., November 11, 1918—Will those who live ever forget that day? Why, the very souls of Canada's sons who lay in Flanders poppy fields rose rejoicing. Our horses and mules seemed to realize that some great event was taking place. Their feeling of nervousness was over, and the increased care bestowed on them gave them confidence.

The entry into Mons was one of triumph. The inhabitants along the route from Jemappes greeted the troops on the march by throwing flowers in their path, some shouting with joy, while others, men and women, wept from the same emotion, and the children followed with a feeling of much longed-for freedom. The horses were not forgotten, for during the halts the inhabitants patted them freely.

The throats of the deliverers filled at these sights. It was a day of great excitement, and the fact of having the enemy on the run and completely vanquished, was a victory won.

The parade and reception in the city of Mons itself was a wonderful ovation. Every window and roof was filled to capacity with citizens of that historic town, who welcomed the Canadian commander and his troops in a manner not surpassed even by the entry of a monarch. Here, to all intents and purposes, our activities ceased and peace-time paint and polish took the place of war. Part of the Canadian Corps advanced into Germany as far as the Rhine. Their rapid advance caused many hardships to both men and horses from exposure and short rations, but once the lines of communication were repaired, the latter at least was overcome and they settled down in the enemy's country until returned to Belgium for the purpose of demobilization and reunion, in the case of the men, with their loved ones.

CHAPTER 4

Cavalry Brigade

The Canadian Cavalry Brigade, divorced as it were from the Canadian Corps, was attached to the British Cavalry Corps, who in the fateful days of the autumn of 1914 held the German advance, and with the first few thousand prevented the taking of the Channel ports. The Canadian brigade won their laurels in subsequent engagements and their gallant deeds will go down into history as some of the greatest achievements ever performed by mounted troops in the Great War.

It is admitted that the use of mounted troops was limited in France and Belgium, but one cannot overlook the fact that Lord Allenby won his laurels by his remarkable ability in the manoeuvring of cavalry, and the day has not yet arrived when the use of cavalry can be dispensed with.

Because horses will travel where tanks cannot, and because war has not been made impossible by increased armaments, cavalry will still play a very important role in the successful issue of any campaign.

The composition of the Canadian Cavalry Brigade included Royal Canadian Horse Artillery, Royal Canadian Dragoons, Lord Strathcona's Horse (R.C.), Fort Garry Horse, Mounted Machine Gun Squadron, Seventh Canadian Field Ambulance, and Cavalry Mobile Veterinary Section. The first engagement of this brigade was at Bazentin le Grand, when they fought beside Indian cavalry and struck terror into the hearts of the Germans.

The former, the Germans stated, never took prisoners alive, while the latter sometimes scalped those who fell into their hands. A long period elapsed between this and their next encounter, "Delville Wood," 1916. They took the field with the newly invented tanks, and charged and sabred a German battery crew. The lull of inactivity which followed this action did not mar the Canadian horsemen's spirits, and in March, 1917, the unexpected happened. The retirement of the German line in front of Peronne gave them their opportunity, and in face of sleet and rain storms they pushed the retiring Germans until Ypres, Equancourt, Longavesnes, Etricourt and Guyencourt fell into the hands of the Strathconas and Fort Garrys, while it is recorded that the Royal Canadian Dragoons captured a whole German Brigade Staff.

During the attack on March 27th, 1917, by Lord Strathcona's Horse on a village, "Guyencourt," a party of the enemy took up a position in a wired trench and opened rapid fire and machine gun fire at a close range, causing heavy casualties in the leading troop of the regiment. Lieut. Harvey, who was in command of the troop of the regiment, ran forward ahead of his men and dashed at the trench, still fully manned, jumped the wire, shot the machine gunner and captured the gun. For this most conspicuous bravery and devotion to duty, Harvey was awarded the V.C., and thereby added another heroic deed to the Canadian Cavalry exploits in the Great War.

The next important mounted engagement came in November, 1917, at Cambrai, when the Fort Garry Horse achieved one of the greatest cavalry exploits of the war. Following the tanks, they climbed the slopes of the Hindenburg Line south of Havrincourt Wood and disposed of the German machine gun nests, and with the tanks still left in action, dashed through the barbed wire and made a heroic and thrilling charge on the St. Quentin Canal, taking on the strongly held villages of Marcoing and Masnieres and ending in the capture of the German army commander in his own headquarters and the surrender of four hundred prisoners.

Lieutenant H. Strachan, M.C., commanded this squadron, and being cut off from all communication, and not knowing what was required of him, pushed forward six miles into the German position, which set the enemy's retreat into a panic. This gallant officer and his men met their greatest adventure just on the outskirts of the village of Rumilly, where they came suddenly upon a German battery firing over open sights. Without a moment's hesitation, Lieutenant Strachan gave the order to charge and the horsemen of our prairies rode down the battery crew, killing every man with their sabres. Later, word was received from their brigade commander that the main objective had been cancelled. With this information to hand, they undauntedly fought their way back to their lines on foot, having first stampeded their horses further into the German lines. For this act the gallant Strachan was awarded the V.C.

On March 25th and 26th, 1918, the Canadians were north of Lagny, and, joining with the French forces, they drove the enemy from the banks of the Canal du Nord on the morning of the 27th.

Mounted, Lieutenant F. M. W. Harvey, V.C, M.C., of the Lord Strathcona's Horse, rode forward with his patrol to Fontaine, and charged the village from the German side, taking a large number of prisoners. The French having planned an attack for the same time, found on their arrival Lieutenant Harvey in possession, and, suspecting that Harvey and his party were Germans in British uniforms, arrested them, and only released them after the French Headquarters had been communicated with as to their identity. For this heroic work Harvey was awarded the M.C. and the French *Croix de Guerre*.

This brings us back to the Amiens Sector, where our cavalry added fresh laurels to Canada's glorious name. On the afternoon of the 29th March, 1918, the Canadian Cavalry Brigade were billeted in the village close to Montdidier. About four p.m. the brigade was ordered with all speed north to protect Amiens, and arrived about two a.m. on the 30th at Bois de Boves, where they rested for two hours. Information was received that all com-

Lance against lance in the Battle of the Marne

Charge of the 9th Lancers at Mortel, September 7th 1914.

ed squadron had cleared the wood northwest of them, when they worked their way back to the woods under very heavy fire to join Lieutenant Harvey's troop. They found that Harvey had had by no means an easy task, as he had lost one-half of his troop and had been forced to fight a hand to hand battle, and, to make matters worse, had been severely wounded himself.

Lieutenant Harvey received a bar to his M.C. for this action, and Lieutenant Flowerdew was awarded a posthumous V.C. for his gallant work, while Lieutenant Brown added to his fame. Of the total number of one hundred and fifty horses that entered into the fray, only four survived.

Amiens—Here our Canadian Cavalry distinguished themselves and came into their own. They protected the Canadian right flank, operating with tanks. On the night of August 6th they moved rapidly and secretly into Amiens, and on the morning of August 8th they were riding over the German trenches to the north of Amiens-Roye road, fighting side by side with their kith, and linking up with the French Thirty-first Corps. Before noon they were heavy in action in front of Weincourt and Beaucourt, taking and capturing a General and his Staff at Fresnoy, who were obviously not aware of the swiftness of their approach. Further to the north of Roye Road, the Royal Canadian Dragoons rounded up a large number of prisoners. The Lord Strathcona's Horse, with the Canadian armoured cars, dashed to the slopes of the village of Le Quesnel and broke up the Germans who were rallying to hold their position. The Fifth Dragoon Guards of the First Cavalry Brigade—Imperials—finally broke through further to the north, to Rosiers, the German rail-head, and there captured a German reinforcing train with some twenty-eight officers and five hundred men and a battery of guns on a railway spur.

During this day of events the cavalry units which participated in this attack travelled nearly thirty-five miles. On August 10th the Canadian Cavalry Brigade was again in action on both sides of the Amiens-Roye road, but was unable to carry out any extensive operations owing to the fact that it had now reached the

munications with the enemy had been lost, and that they were thought to be in the vicinity of Noreuil Woods.

The brigade at this time formed part of the Second Cavalry Division, and moved from Bois de Boves at six a.m. with orders to reconnoitre in the vicinity of Moreuil Woods, and gain touch with the enemy. Crossing the river at Castel, the brigade proceeded south towards Moreuil along the Avre River, and on arrival at a mill between Moreuil Village and the woods it was discovered that the Germans occupied both village and woods.

Two squadrons of the Lord Strathcona's Horse (R.C.), supported by Fort Garry Horse, were ordered to attack the woods dismounted; another squadron Lord Strathcona's Horse was sent mounted to the north-east of the woods, for the purpose of carrying out any action that might be necessary against German reinforcements entering the woods.

"C" Squadron, Lord Strathcona's Horse (R.C.) was commanded by Lieutenant G. M. Flowerdew. On arrival at the extreme north-west corner of the woods, German reinforcements numbering between two and three hundred were observed approaching from the direction of Villers aux Erables. The nearest party of the enemy was about three hundred yards from our squadron. Lieutenant Flowerdew, realizing that he must act quickly in order to prevent these reinforcements entering the woods, detached Lieutenant Harvey, V.C., and his troop to a flank to bring covering fire to bear on the enemy, while he himself led the remaining three troops in a very gallant charge equal in dash to the Light Brigade at Balaclava, charging approximately one hundred Germans with machine guns. After disposing of this force, they routed in real Canadian spirit two smaller parties numbering fifty and seventy-five respectively. The three troops which actually took part in the charge consisted of three officers and seventy-five other ranks. The officers were Lieutenants Brown, Flowerdew, and Tripp, the first named being the only survivor. By this time there were practically no men left mounted, so the surviving officer concentrated his remaining men in an old trench, where they remained until the dismount-

old Somme battlefields, which had been occupied by the Germans from 1914 to 1916, who, by their old trenches and barbed wire, had rendered the ground impossible for cavalry. However, three troops of the Fort Garry Horse attempted an attack on the high ground to the west of the village of Roye, but they were forced to use the road. The Germans having machine guns and rifles trained on this road, prevented the horsemen (although they rode gallantly and as one), from reaching the objective.

On October 9th the brigade went into action from Maretz across the battlefields where the Imperial Cavalry Regiments fought so gallantly in 1914. They took their objective, which was the high ground north of the town of Le Cateau, and gained a footing in Le Cateau itself, as well as the villages of Montay and Neuvilly-Inchy. The Germans not being able to stand the flashing sabres, surrendered in large numbers.

At Catignay Wood, where there was a concentration of German machine guns, the Fort Garrys charged straight at the guns, killing most of the crew and capturing the rest.

In another case the Strathconas took on fifteen German machine guns. The fire was terrible, but the troops, sabres glittering, charged forward, with the result that the German gunners fled, leaving their guns.

The reception given the Canadian plainsmen as they galloped through the streets of the occupied villages was a greeting never to be forgotten. Townsfolk who had been under the iron fist of the German rule rushed from their homes to meet the horsemen from the Canadian plains.

Women pulled officers and men from their mounts and put their arms around the necks of the men and horses, as a mark of appreciation for their deliverance and liberty. The inhabitants strewed flowers on the path and freely offered wine and coffee to our men to the tune of the machine guns of a retiring enemy. Such, then, is the price of liberty and the mortal part played by the man and the horse in war.

I only recount these great events to depict just what the life of the cavalry horse is in battle, and the reader, I am sure, will picture such horses in their endeavour to carry their masters to victory.

On April 3, 1918, General Rawlinson, when addressing the Cavalry Brigade, said that their failure to capture Moreuil Woods, which they had retaken, would have been fatal to the defence of Amiens.

"Your courage and determination have turned the fortunes of the day," he declared.

Such sentiments were extended to both men and horses, I feel sure, for the horses bore their riders to fame, made possible only by their faithfulness.

"GOODBYE, OLD MAN"
An incident on the road to a Battery Position
in Southern Flanders.

CHAPTER 5

Veterinary Corps

The Veterinary Corps—R.A.V.C. and C.A.V.C.—under the direct and able administration of Major-General Sir John Moore, the D.V.S. of all British Forces in France and Belgium, rendered excellent services. It is not my intention to dilate on this particular service to any great extent other than to show in as few words as possible how animals in their days of trial were cared for by that corps.

Let us start from the Regimental Veterinary Officer. Each infantry, artillery and cavalry brigade had detailed to it a veterinary officer who attended to the medical care of the animals of his brigade; he kept well forward during the battle where his services were most urgently required, dressing wounds and treating minor ailments and evacuating any serious cases to what was known as the Mobile Veterinary Section.

In the event of an injured or wounded animal not being able to walk to the Mobile Veterinary Section, it was the veterinary officer's duty to inform the officer commanding the section of the circumstance. The officer in turn would order the ambulance to proceed to the given location on the map and pick up the animal so reported, which would then be taken to the Mobile Veterinary Section for further treatment, and later, if found necessary, evacuated to a base hospital.

During battle advanced aid posts were supervised by regimental veterinary officers detailed by the D.A.D.V.S.'s Division. Such posts acted as advanced dressing stations did for men; here wounded animals received first aid before proceeding to their respective lines or directly to the Mobile Veterinary Section.

During the Passchendaele action we had advanced aid posts at Spree Farm, where very heroic services under terrific shell fire and bombing and other adverse conditions, were rendered by the veterinary officer in charge. This officer dressed the wounded animals which were returning from the battery positions over fascine-made roads, and humanely destroyed those beyond medical assistance. For this work Captain Matthews received the Belgian *Croix de Guerre*.

Leaving the regimental veterinary officer, we may consider the Mobile Veterinary Section. The Mobile Veterinary Section was always a busy spot; the ambulances or floats were kept going day and night. In battle this unit was located as far forward as possible from the Veterinary Evacuation Station, which would be situated generally at corps rail-head. Its duty, to be efficient, was to receive all such injured animals from units and to get rid of the serious cases by sending them to base hospitals through the Veterinary Evacuation Station, where more favourable conditions for treatment were available, while the minor cases were retained, treated, and returned to their original units in the course of a few days. They also collected from the forward areas serious cases which were unable to walk; in short, their policy was to take over all animals which tended to impede the mobility of the units within the division to which they were attached.

It was, therefore, a very important unit, and the officer in charge required a great deal of judgment in selecting his cases for evacuation to the base. All animals were accompanied by an evacuation roll giving a serial number, description, name of unit to which they belonged, and the reason for which they were evacuated, together with a special descriptive label attached to the head-collar of each animal, "White" for medical cases, "Green" for surgical, "Red" for mange or other communicable diseases.

Apart from these details, for identification purposes, the designation of the Mobile Veterinary Section or Veterinary Evacua-

MOBILE VETERINARY SECTION
A four-footed casualty. Bandaging a horse hit by shrapnel.

tion Station, and serial number of the case was stencilled on the rump of the animal so that identification became very easy. This permitted a check on contagious diseases amongst animals, for all animals on arrival at the Reception Veterinary Hospital were submitted to the Mallein test for glanders, and if animals were found to react steps were immediately taken to communicate with the division from which it came, so as to prevent the spread of the disease by testing all animals within that unit.

At Amiens the work of our mobile veterinary sections brought forth great praise. One veterinary officer whose section was continually being bombed day and night, constantly moved his section with a view to lessening the casualties, and in doing so was wounded himself, but remained on duty. The fact of this officer being wounded on three other occasions and his heroic work in this particular battle won for him an immediate award of the Military Cross. This sustained loyalty to duty by officers commanding mobile veterinary sections was general, and a great deal of appreciation was extended to them by their higher commands.

The Veterinary Evacuation Stations, which constituted the next link in the chain of responsibility of carrying out the evacuation of veterinary cases, were situated in close vicinity to corps rail-head. This was a very necessary unit in a war such as the Great War. Its duties chiefly comprised the receiving from the Mobile Veterinary Section of all their battle casualties as well as sick and injured and the forwarding of these animals on to the base hospital by railroad or canal barge, thereby assisting the officer commanding the mobile veterinary section to keep his section cleared and permitting him to move with his division at all times.

This unit also had as part of its equipment a motor horse ambulance, capable of transporting two animals. This, however, was not supplied until later in the war, but for the period it was in use proved very useful in assisting the mobile veterinary sections in transporting their serious cases to rail-head for evacuation.

The veterinary evacuation section also assisted in collecting any animals which were unable to proceed on account of injury or weakness, and had been left on the line of march by the different divisions of the corps. The most effectual means of evacuating animals from the forward areas was by returning supply trains from divisional rail-heads. It permitted animals to arrive at the reception veterinary hospitals on lines of communication more quickly and in better condition, which was most essential for the expeditious treatment of wounds and diseases and also for general economy, as utilizing such trains lessened the congestion of traffic on roads during an offensive operation.

This means of evacuation was not always possible, for often removal by road had to be resorted to in so far as walking cases were concerned, and by motor ambulance for the more serious cases. Walking cases were tied in pairs to long ropes, one on each side, about twenty in number, with a man guiding the leading pair, another at the end of the rope, and a third man in the middle. This means of conducting horses and mules to rear areas proved satisfactory under the circumstances, especially in view of assistance rendered by the motor ambulances, which, I am told, numbered twenty-five, placed at the disposal of the veterinary service by the Royal Society for the Prevention of Cruelty to Animals.

The method of evacuating animals by canal barge was the most novel means adopted, besides being a most restful procedure for such patients. Each barge carried thirty-two animals, and was drawn by horse power, the journey occupying about seven to ten hours in all. The task of feeding the wounded and debilitated animals on such journeys, particularly by train, was attended to by suitable men detailed from the evacuating units. One private to each car, with a non-commissioned officer in charge of the party, accompanied the animals on the train, and sufficient rations for the men and the animals on the journey were drawn through the supply officer at the rail-head. Water was carried both in cartridge cases of large calibre shells and empty biscuit or petrol tins. The former method was the most practical and useful because for feeding and watering arrange-

A PATIENT ENTERING AN AMBULANCE

ments on the train it obviated any demand *en route*, and lessened the trouble both for the horses and the men.

VETERINARY BASE HOSPITALS.

Few realize the amount of work performed by the veterinary hospitals in time of war, and as the saying goes, "No one wants a sick horse," so these hospitals were the home of refuge for the horse and the mule when not serviceable in other places.

As a considerable amount of sickness appeared in overseas remounts newly arrived in the theatre of war, veterinary hospitals were located on lines of communication, usually near large remount depots, with a view to minimizing the transportation of cases from such depots; while other hospitals were conveniently situated at centres forward of the main area and easily accessible from forward areas. These hospitals, each with a personnel of six hundred and thirty, which included ten veterinary officers, thirty-three farriers and seventy other non-commissioned officers, were desired, organized and equipped for the skilled treatment and comfort of the patients, and provided for approximately two thousand sick animals.

The buildings consisted chiefly of stabling, constructed of wood and galvanized iron, and they were laid out in blocks of two hundred and fifty standings, with thirty-five feet between each standing; these spaces were seeded down to grass, which was fed to the patients. The green effect of the spaces presented a very artistic appearance. Each standing had its own dressing sheds, forage, watering troughs, etc., so that any contagious disease, in the event of an outbreak, could be controlled with less difficulty. Forage stores were also provided at the ends of each line.

Stable floors were built of bricks, stones, cobbles, planking, cement, all of which served the purpose of keeping the animals dry and out of the mire, which was a very essential factor in the treatment of wounds and injuries, more especially of those of the lower extremities.

The function of a veterinary hospital, then, was to be ready at all times, night or day, to receive the animals evacuated by the different divisional mobile veterinary sections and evacuating stations, and to bring about the greatest economy in animal wastage by medical, surgical and restorative treatment.

In such hospitals there were three sections: reception, mange and general. The patients were first received at the reception hospital, and there subjected to the Mallein test for glanders; in the event of the test being negative the animals were inspected and despatched to one of the other sections, and there treated according to the nature of their maladies. Those considered hopeless were, after inspection by higher authority, disposed of. Surgical cases received immediate attention, and it was a common sight to see three to six animals under the influence of anaesthetic, undergoing operations under the skilled hand of the veterinary officer.

The usual procedure was to transfer the medical and the surgical cases to the general section, where the former could receive the necessary treatment and the latter the after treatment.

Mange cases, of course, were sent to the mange section, where they underwent a series of dipping by running them through vats containing calcium sulphate solution. This method of treatment went a long way towards keeping this disease under control.

Debility cases, which required little treatment, other than good nursing and hygiene, were sent to what was known as a convalescent horse depot, where they were rested and nursed back to normal health. As time went on, these horses would be again transferred to remount depots, and from there returned to the divisions.

It was a common sight to see old pals back again, while men often recognized horses they had known on the Canadian ranges, which they had assisted to break prior to the outbreak of the war. Again, horses recognized the voices of old masters.

One particular horse named Billy, whose master. Colonel W. MacDermott, C.A.M.C., was evacuated sick, but later returned to the brigade just when the unit was being broken up as a mounted formation, was placed among the horses set apart to

A Veterinary Hospital

be absorbed by other units. The colonel was anxious to see Billy again, and started to walk down the line, shouting "Billy." The result was surprising; the horse recognized the voice, and immediately began to neigh, and shortly after exhibited great joy at seeing his old master again.

Of this very important branch of the service, the following figures, which cover the period August 18, 1914, to January 23, 1919, will give an idea of the magnitude of its work:

HOSPITAL CASES

Admitted	725,216
Cured	529,064
Died	18,975
Destroyed	127,741
Sold	29,524
Remaining	19,912

BATTLE CASUALTIES FROM JULY 1, 1916, TO NOVEMBER 11, 1918

Gas—Succumbed to gas	210
Affected	2,200

WOUNDED—SHELL, BULLET AND BOMBS

Killed	58,090
Wounded	77,410
Total Casualties	137,960

It was an enormous undertaking to treat and nurse such large numbers of animals back to health.

Great precautionary measures were adopted to prevent horses picking up wire nails which were dumped on the main travelled roads, either by cooks emptying ashes or by quartermaster-sergeants breaking up boxes.

The divisions were responsible for greatly reducing our casualties in this connection either by tacking up posters which pointed out the seriousness of permitting nails to lie around; or by placing boxes on fence walls for the deposition of nails found by men on the road. Some divisions put men out for the purpose of collecting nails and other sharp pieces of iron which were liable to be picked up by the feet of horses travelling on the roads.

It will be of interest to note that the total number of horses affected by nail punctures within the British forces in France numbered as many as four hundred in one week.

Horse Shows.

Departing from the general routine of war, one outstanding feature which went a long way towards encouraging individuals in the care of animals was the horse show. To some these shows appeared to be unnecessary, but to those who were able to follow the benefits derived from them the results were appreciated, as they greatly improved the care and management of animals generally within the corps.

Brigade horse shows brought about rivalry between the units and divisional horse shows between brigades, and so on. These brigade horse shows had a tendency to bring the smaller unit horse transport into play, and therefore required units to keep all their animals, harness and wagons up to the mark.

It was gratifying to note the individual care bestowed upon certain teams by their drivers who worked on into the late hours of the night so that they would not be outclassed in the show the following day.

Apart from this aspect they produced a great deal of pleasure to the individual as well as to the officers commanding the lesser units, commanders of brigades, divisions and corps, and it broke the monotony of war conditions.

AN ARMY HOSPITAL
Dressers at work in a hospital of the R.A.V.C

CHAPTER 6

Stories

The reader cannot but realize the diverse difficulties our horses and mules had to overcome, and that shellfire and bombs were not altogether their worst enemy.

The illustrations contained herein will, I trust, serve to depict the terrible road conditions over which man and beast were forced to travel for days unending, bearing every discomfort this world could offer—mud, cold rains, and enemy shell-fire.

The following incidents were related to me just lately by Major Williams. A mule carrying ammunition near Pollcapelle in September, 1917, on the way to the gun-line sank out of sight in a shell-hole. Before ropes could be passed around him, to assist in extricating him from his terrible predicament, it was realized that relief was impossible, so a kindly bullet ended his troubles just before his head went below the sticky surface.

The cut showing a water-cart horse mired illustrates the danger of the road which our horses travelled and the danger of turning off fascine-made roads even for a short distance. The horse in this instance was extricated but the water-cart eventually sank lower and lower until it became part of the road.

A story is told by a gunner of the Royal Horse Artillery of a man who gave his life for a horse. In one of the desperate attacks along the Aisne, a party of ours was nearly cut off, and had to retreat in hot haste. As we cleared out, there was a man of the Gloucestershires who noticed that a horse which had been struck by a shell was in great pain, and was neighing piteously for water. There was none about, and with the Germans rapidly closing in, it was as much as a man's life was worth to stay another minute. This brave chap knew this as well as anyone, but he wanted to make the poor animal comfortable before he cleared off, so he hunted around until he found water. We had to retire, and did not know what happened to him until the next day, when we retook the position, and found the Gloucester lad and the horse both dead.

Not for honours alone will the British soldier risk danger, but with that fine chivalry which is ever at the services of the weak and oppressed, he will, whether a simple private or a commissioned officer, extend his aid to creatures of lesser usefulness.

Major R. S. Timmis, D.S.O., of the Royal Canadian Dragoons, relates the following narrative regarding the cunningness of a mule:

"B" Squadron, Royal Canadian Dragoons, had a very cunning mule. She was one of the Hotchkiss gun pack animals, who, whenever she got under fire, would lie down. One day when the squadron had very heavy casualties in the March Boche push, 1918, and many of the horses were being bowled over by German machine gun fire, this mule lay down in a hollow piece of ground,—her leader had been wounded—and when the firing ceased she got up and rejoined her pals, with all the ammunition on her back.

The major gives a further incident of a horse becoming shell-shocked at Roye, on the French front. The French sappers were blowing up a bridge over the Aisne Canal; a horse of one of our squadrons, the sergeant-major's, got badly shell-shocked from the detonation and went completely mad. The animal rushed about and kicked several men and became so dangerous that it was ordered to be shot. The veterinary officer who witnessed the incident expressed an opinion that the animal's condition was no doubt due to the terrific detonation.

The nervous effect of shelling and bombing on horses and

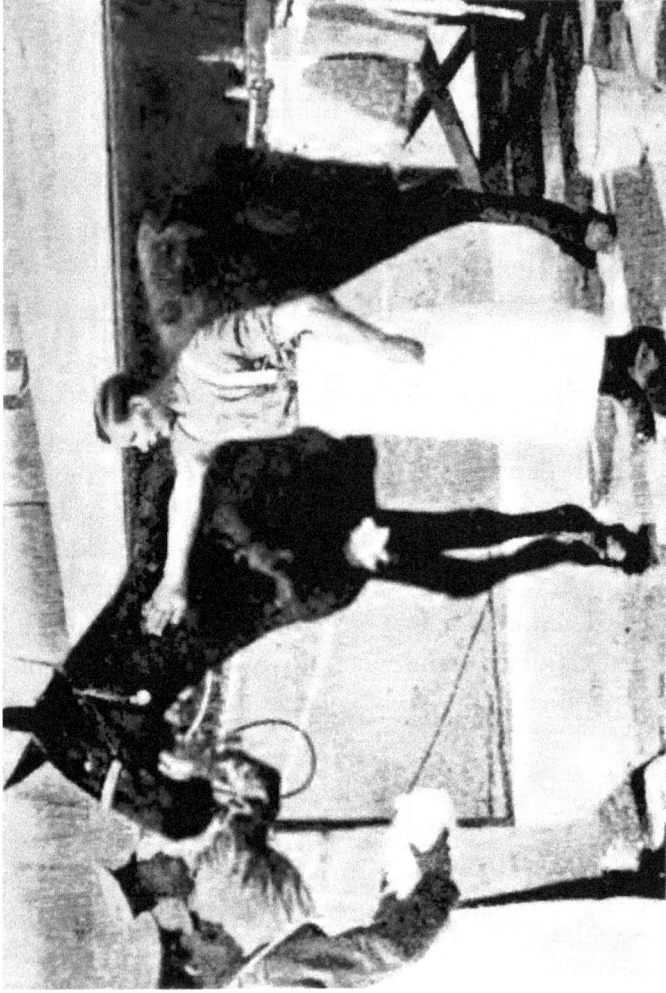

A WOUNDED MULE AT A HOSPITAL

mules was without doubt very evident. I remember the deputy director of remounts for the First Army, Colonel Kennedy Shaw, issuing me a very fine mare, an English thoroughbred type. She was at one time the charger of General Lord Home, the commander of that army.

Upon getting the animal to divisional headquarters I found it necessary to go forward of the field artillery. Directly I reached the vicinity of the guns this mare almost collapsed. I could feel her give from under me, and she broke out in a terrible sweat. I tried to coax her along, but because of the continuous shelling of the enemy and our own field guns, which numbered quite a few hundred, I was unable to reach my destination on her. I therefore dismounted and sent my groom back to the horse lines with her, while I continued on his mount, which apparently did not mind the Huns' right to search our area with his guns.

After this it was impossible for me to use this mare in the forward areas, which so often required my services.

I knew quite a number of horses which were so affected. Most of them were of high nervous temperament and any excitement such as shelling did not assist them.

The instinct of horses recognizing danger points where the enemy had the advantage of direct observation, and which permitted continuous shelling of such points, was most marked.

When passing, horses often exhibited the faculty of remembering previous adventures at such points, and would show alertness or fright. Again, upon returning to stables or standings which had been shelled or bombed they invariably faltered before entering, as much as to say to their masters, "Do you think this is safe?" or "Don't you think the enemy are likely to hand us a few more presents if we go in there?" A feeling of anxiety always came over them directly shelling or bombing took place, and their masters often had to persuade them with words of kindness that nothing was wrong, at which they would bow to the will of man and enter as if to say, "Well, I will take your word that you will protect me."

A wounded horse or mule, to my mind, always wore an expression of gratefulness when those who endeavoured to alleviate his pains were attending him, or when his master was bidding a last farewell to his mortally wounded pal. This is depicted in the picture, "Goodbye, Old man." by F. Matinia, which "The Sphere" reproduced in one of its issues and which is included in this book; one cannot imagine a more pathetic incident of friendship between man and horse than this picture depicts. The look of anxiety on the horse's face and the man's feeling in having to leave his pal on the modern field of battle, a feeling no lover of animals can suppress in times of war or peace, appeal to every one's sympathy, and many a heartfelt sore and many a tear fell when man left his dumb pal under dire circumstances.

"MIRED"

This picture illustrates the danger of turning off a fascine road. The water in this particular incident eventually sank from sight and became part of the road. Picture desolate conditions.

CHAPTER 7

Exhibits

Major A. E. Cameron, M.C., C.A.V.C, compiled the following short history of twenty-one wounded Canadian horses which is most interesting and which will give the reader a slight idea of a veterinary officer's work in the field.

It must be observed that a great deal of the surgical work performed on horses would be in the medical profession considered major operations, while in veterinary surgery such operations are rendered minor with the aid of a local anaesthetic.

Photograph and history of fragments and bullets removed from Canadian horses in the Great War. Reading from left to right along each line from the top:

(1) Rifle bullet fired from an aeroplane, hitting a heavy draft horse belonging to the 27th Infantry Battalion; extracted 17.8.18.

(2) Machine bullet extracted from the jaw of a light draft horse belonging to the 28th Infantry Battalion, 1.10.18.

(3) History unknown.

(4) German rifle bullet extracted from a wound in horse; detail lost.

(5) Automatic pistol bullet entered the forehead of a horse belonging to 2nd Canadian Division Headquarters Police. This animal was destroyed on account of its foot being shattered by shell. After death this bullet was extracted from the point of shoulder.

(6) Shrapnel lead bullet extracted from between the ribs

of a riding horse belonging to the 5th Canadian Machine Gun Company.

(7) Shrapnel lead bullet extracted from the foreleg of a horse belonging to the 5th Canadian Machine Gun Company, near Ypres, 6.11.17.

(8) Exhibit No. 8 was removed from the tail of a light draft horse belonging to the 5th Canadian Machine Gun Company during the battle of Passchendaele, 6.11.17.

(9) This fragment was extracted from a wound which had penetrated seven inches in the vicinity of the backbone, 3.9.17.

(10) This fragment of a bomb wounded two horses at Reninghelst; other fragments of this same bomb wounded five men and also passed through the veterinary officer's hut.

(11) Fragment which hit a heavy draft horse on the off side of neck, 5.10.18, passing through the elastic ligament previous to 16.10.18. This fragment could not be felt, as a probe would not pass through the ligament; however, a small collection of pus made its location and extraction easy.

(12) Portion of a bomb removed from a wound in the back of a horse belonging to the 28th Infantry Battalion. 19.7.18.

(13) This fragment was removed from the tail of the charger "Topsy," wounded at Guillaucourt, August, 1918. This horse was ridden by Brigadier-General A. H. Bell, C.M.G., D.S.O.

(14) This fragment was extracted from a horse belonging to the 31st Infantry Battalion in the near jaw, wound 1½ inches deep, with profuse haemorrhage, 17.9.18.

(15) This fragment was removed from the inside of the nostril of a horse belonging to the 28th Infantry Battalion, June, 1917. The fragment had been embedded for three months, and the fact not having been reported, was only ascertained after questioning the driver on account of

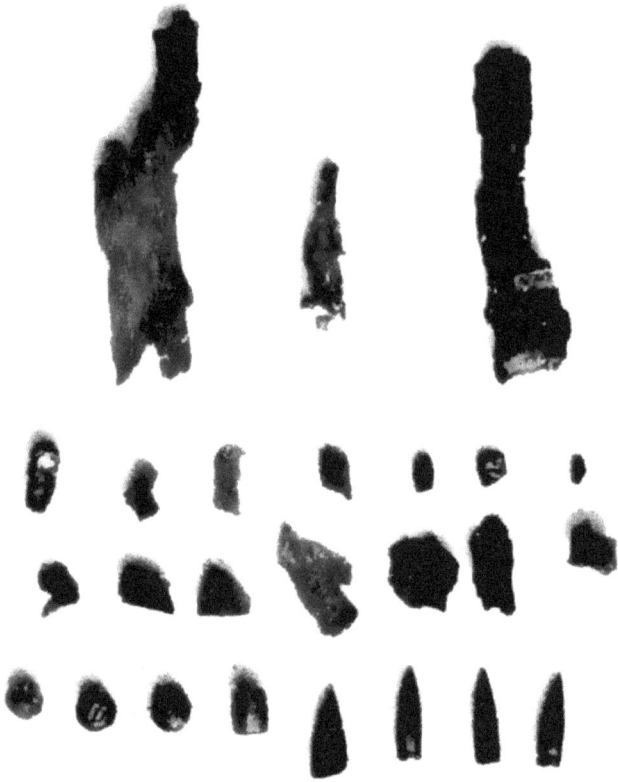

FRAGMENTS AND BULLETS EXTRACTED FROM
WOUNDED HORSES

symptoms which were presented later.

(16) Fragment extracted from the lower jawbone of a horse belonging to the 20th Battery, C.F.A., 15.8.17. This piece proved very difficult to remove.

(17) This piece of a high explosive shell wounded a horse belonging to the 14th Canadian Machine Gun Company, in the face and tongue, smashing the tusk tooth, and later was extracted from the tongue, 8.8.17.

(18) Bomb fragment extracted with three other pieces from a light draft horse belonging to the 28th Infantry Battalion, from a wound two inches deep in the neck.

(19) This larger fragment hit the forearm, travelling around under the skin. An incision was made and the piece was removed from the other side of the leg, 31.8.18.

(20) Exhibit No. 20 was removed from the shoulder of a horse belonging to the 5th Brigade, C.F.A., 18.8.17. This bit of shrapnel passed upwards and inwards six inches.

(21) Exhibit No. 21 remained in the thigh of a horse belonging to the 6th Field Company, Canadian Engineers for seven months, and was extracted 4.4.18.

(22) Fragment removed from the neck of a horse belonging to the 31st Battalion, 7.11.17, wound four inches deep. This same bomb killed two officers and two men as well as wounding four others at Ypres, 7.11.17.

The history of the three large pieces shown at the bottom of the plate is not available. All the above exhibits are photographs.

VETERINARY LINES
1st Canadian Mounted Rifles.

CHAPTER 8

Horses and Photographs

Our horses and mules, as there was no home for them, did not return, with the exception of a few privileged ones, one hundred and ten, which were the chargers of senior officers. These horses were returned to Canada, and were cared for by their masters in a befitting manner. Photographs of a few out-standing horses will be seen here, many of which still bear the battle marks of Flanders, having been wounded as many as three times.

The senior officers were all excellent horsemen, and the interest they took in their horses was second only to that exhibited on behalf of their men. They always had a word of appreciation for men who showed interest in the care of their horses. This went a long way to promote efficiency in animal management in the field. They were also very keen to detect faults in that connection.

Few know even at this time what happened to the majority of Canadian horses and mules—twenty-four thousand odd—which was the approximate strength at the time of the Armistice. Many statements have been made as to their disposal, but I can assure my readers that most of them found fitting homes. These were not rest homes entirely, for their labour was not over and their task of assisting the re-establishment of Belgium was a very important one. They were made use of on farms, around mines, and in industrial work generally.

All our Canadian horses, with the exception of the few that

THEIR LAST TRIP
Ammunition team killed by shell fire in the forward area.

returned to Canada, were sold to the Belgian government, who in turn disposed of them by auction within the great centres of that country. So physically fit and free from disease were our horses and mules that not one was rejected by the representatives of Belgium, which fact was certainly a feather in the caps of the Canadian troops who were responsible for their care.

Canada owes to the dumb animals a great deal of gratitude and appreciation for the magnificent part they played in the Great War. This duty was done without a murmur, and the horse, with his co-partner, man, was in part responsible for victory.

GENERAL SIR A.W. CURRIE, C.G.M.G., K.C.B. AND HIS STAFF AT THE EAST END OF THE BONN BRIDGE CROSSING INTO GERMANY AT THE HEAD OF THE 1ST CANADIAN INFANTRY BATTALION

Famous Canadian War Horses

General Sir Arthur Currie took command of the Canadian Corps and led his men to victory with minimum casualties.

"Barrage Currie," as he was known at the First Army Headquarters, on account of his persistency in demanding an artillery barrage to protect his men in battle; his first thoughts were for his men and next for his horses. The triumph that followed his taking over command of the corps will never die in the annals of Canadian history. The corps commander was not only the master-mind of the corps, but his spirit of justice and high sense of duty inspired those who served under him. In short, he was a genius of no mean distinction, a born leader of men and a lover of dumb animals.

"Brocklebank"

One of the famous horses to take part in the Great War was "Brocklebank," the charger of General Sir A. W. Currie, C.G.M.G., K.C.B. This bay gelding, originally called "British Hero," and commonly known as "Brock," was imported by Mr. S. L. Howe, of Vancouver, B.C., in 1912.. He was a hackney-bred animal and a winner of many blue ribbons, both in this country and in England. He was greatly admired for his style and conformation.

Upon declaration of war in 1914, Mr. Howe very generously presented "British Hero"—"Brock"—and his mate, "Erin's Pride," to the Dominion Government.

When "British Hero" arrived at Valcartier, P.Q., he was selected by General Currie for use as his personal charger and

General Sir Arthur W. Currie, G.C.M.G., K.C.B.
Mounted on his famous Charger, "British Hero."
commonly known as "Brocklebank."

"BROCKLEBANK"
The Charger of General Sir Arthur W. Currie,
G.C.M.G., K.C.B.

given the name of "Brocklebank." This horse was one of the first to take the field and the last to leave.

No horse was more outstanding in the Great War than this animal. He stood the rigours of the campaign in the most splendid fashion, but he had one peculiarity—he had a mind of his own. Sometimes he disagreed with the general who was riding him, and undertook to rough-ride him for a few minutes or so, but this sulkiness did not last long.

Sir Arthur rode "Brocklebank" at all the principal parades which he attended—the reviews by His Majesty the King, in England and France—on the Field Marshal's reviews.

When the troops crossed the Bonn Bridge this horse led the Canadian troops into Germany at the head of the Third Battalion.

"Brocklebank" became famous like his master, one a great leader of men, the other a leader in the equine world.

At the termination of the war this famous charger found a home on the farm of General Sir Arthur Currie's brother in Western Ontario, where the general goes very often. In the words of the general; "I visit my old home about three times a year, and am always glad to know that he "Brock"—recognizes me; he immediately comes up to me. and smells around my pockets for apples or some other sweets."

A picture of appreciation and good comradeship could not, to my mind, be better painted.

"CASEY."

"Casey," bay gelding, the charger of Lt.-General Sir A. C. Macdonell, K.C.B.. C.M.G., D.S.O., Commanding First Canadian Division, was famous in many ways. Like his master, "Casey" was a warrior bold. He was the only original charger of the old Strathconas which proceeded to France on May 4, 1915, when the Canadian Cavalry Brigade went over. His master loved and rode him continuously during those long years of the war.

General Macdonell delighted to put "Casey" through the many tricks he had taught him.

"CASEY"
The Charger of Lt.-General Sir A. Macdonell,
K.C.B., C.M.G., D.S.O.

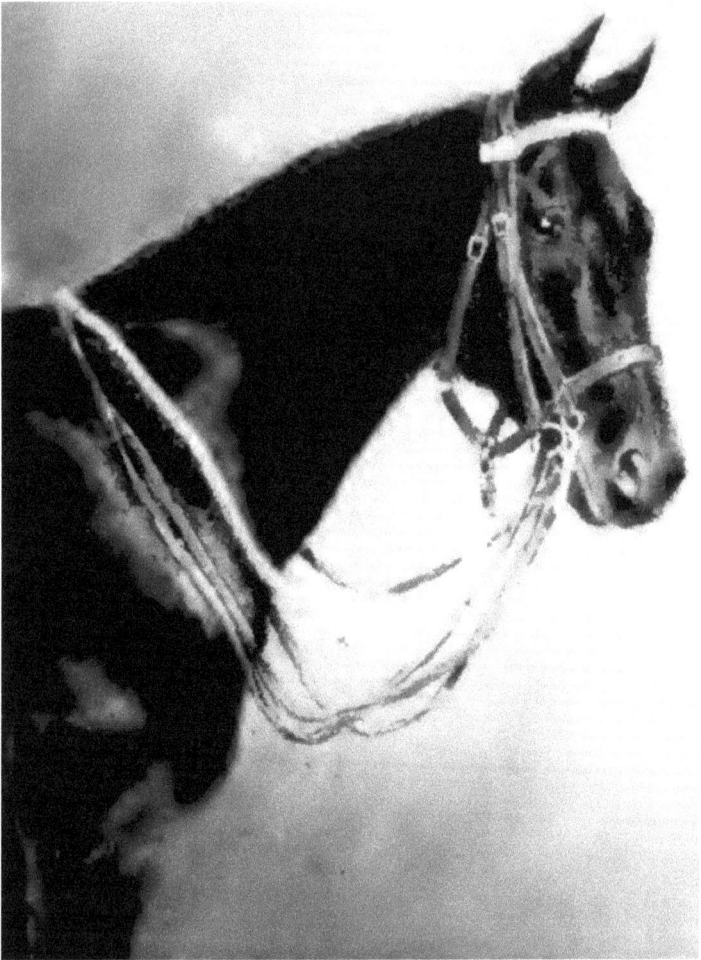

"BAD GIRL"
The Charger of Major-General J. H. MacBrien,
C.B., C.M.G., D.S.O.

He served with the Strathconas, the Seventh Canadian Infantry Brigade, and with the First Division, winding up by carrying his master into Germany on the famous triumphant march following the Armsitice. In short, "Casey" was most popular, and was known to practically all within the units he served.

"Casey" was returned to Canada, and continued to serve his master at the Royal Military College, Kingston, Ontario, where he died. "Casey" was buried in the college grounds, and the inscription on the stone which lies over the spot where this noble animal rests reads as follows:

CASEY

For 18 years my faithful charger in peace and war, died on duty April 2nd, 1925, age 29 years.

A. C. Macdonell.

"JULIA FRANCES" AND "BAD GIRL."

The charger of Major-General J. H. MacBrien, C.B., C.M.G., D.S.O., "Julia Frances," an Irish-bred mare, ridden by General MacBrien for three years of the war, was badly wounded towards the latter end of the campaign, but returned to duty shortly before the Armistice, This beautiful creature is branded "J. F.," and for this reason the general called her after his mother, "Julia Frances."

The second charger of General MacBrien, "Bad Girl," an English-bred mare, was famous for her grace of carriage. The general himself mentions that she had enough devilment, as her name indicates, for half a dozen horses. "Bad Girl" was the winner of many blue ribbons in France, and was greatly admired by all who knew her. She was never sick or sorry, and went through the war from start to finish with the Canadian troops.

Both chargers were brought back to Canada, and are now serving with the Royal Canadian Dragoons, Toronto, (as at time of first publication).

"KING."

"King," dark bay gelding, Major-General Sir Edward Morrison's charger, was bred by Mr. Sloy in the Niagara peninsula. A

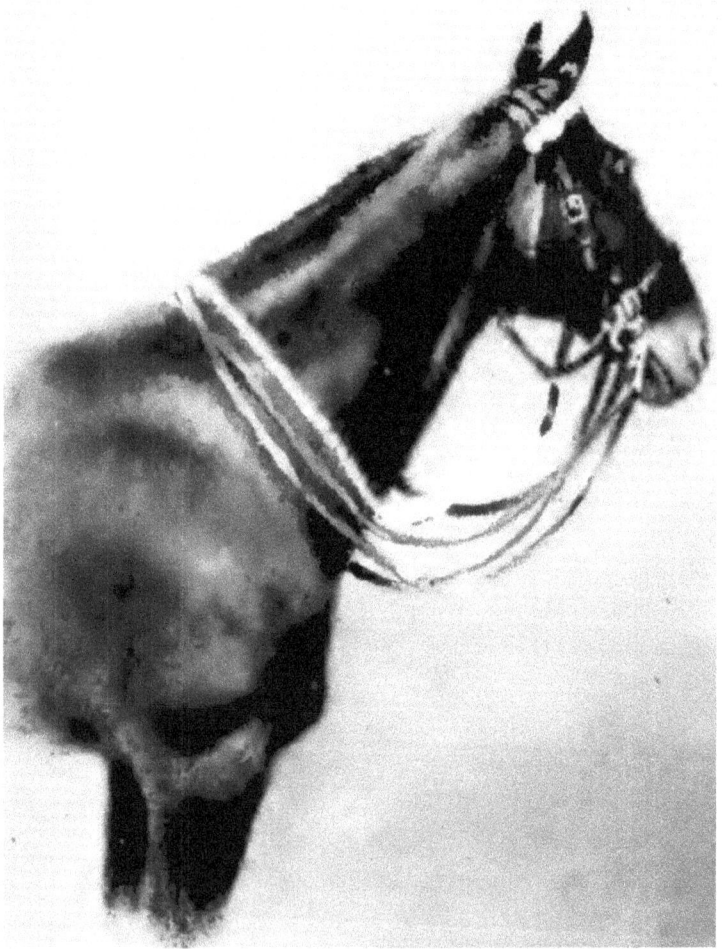

"JULIA FRANCES"
The second Charger of Major-Gen. J. H. MacBrien,
C.B., C.M.G., D.S.O.

"KING"
The Charger of Major-Gen. Sir E. W. B. Morrison,
K.C.M.G., C.B., D.S.O.

splendid weight carrier, being about 15.3 hands with thorough-bred and coach strain.

The general bought him in 1909, and trained him himself, especially as his own charger. This horse was awarded three first prizes at Ottawa Horse Show. "King" crossed to England in the fall of 1914, with the First Canadian Division, and came through the rigorous winter of 1914 and 1915 on Salisbury Plain; was present at the second battle of Ypres, where he was subjected to the gas attack on the afternoon of April 22, 1915.

With his master he followed the fortunes of the Canadian Corps. He became thoroughly inured to shell fire, and such a well-trained charger that nothing would shake his nerve or daunt him. Under battle conditions, burning villages, the explosion of "booby traps," or the bursting of bombs in the vicinity, he would not exhibit fright or nervousness.

In 1920 "King," by permission of the Government, was returned to Canada, and landed at Montreal. He eventually reached his home in Ottawa, where he was well-known and received a welcome befitting a veteran soldier that had been through every battle, march and siege of the war, from Neuve Chapelle to the capture of Mons, including Ypres, Amiens, Passchendaele, the march into Germany, and occupation of the Rhine.

After his return home the old war horse was pensioned on a farm not far from Ottawa, owned by a farmer who as a young man had served as a driver under General Morrison in "D" Battery during the South African war. There he died the following year on April 22nd, the anniversary of the second Battle of Ypres.

There never was a better stamp of war horse; full of fire, with considerable speed, notwithstanding his weight; as already said, afraid of nothing; carrying himself proudly, and with an air of readiness to trample down all before him; indeed, as an admirer once said of him, "He seemed fit to carry a Caesar and his fortunes."

"GEORGE."

"George," the charger of Major-General H. Panet, C.B.,

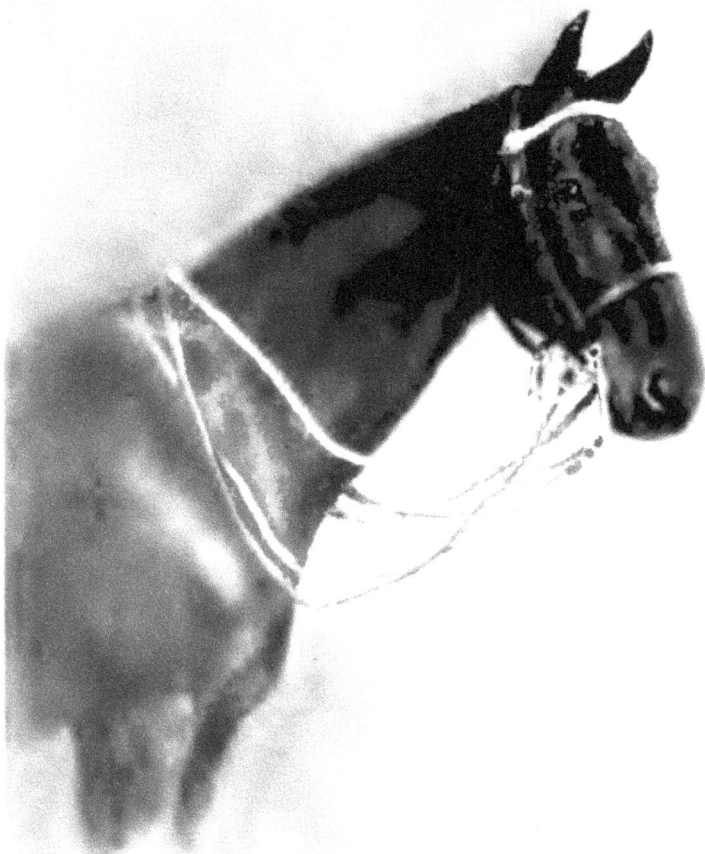

"George"
The Charger of Major-General H. Panet,
C.B., C.M.G., D.S.O.

C.M.G., D.S.O., was a bay gelding, purchased in Ontario in 1909. He was taken overseas in 1914 and served throughout the Great War.

George was severely wounded at Thelus on Vimy Ridge, during the latter part of April, 1917, and was evacuated to Base Veterinary Hospital, and returned in about six weeks to duty.

This animal was noted for his jumping ability, and carried off many blue ribbons in this respect, and was well known throughout the whole of the Canadian Corps.

His reputation within the Second Canadian Divisional Artillery was next to his master, being ever ready for the fray and dauntless in the execution of any duty he had to face; in fact, it is recorded that George feared nothing.

"Topsy."

The charger of Major-General A. H. Bell, C.M.G., D.S.O., Commanding the Sixth Canadian Infantry Brigade, with its master, was one of the first to go to France from Western Canada.

She was an Alberta bred animal, and was noted for her great endurance and splendid disposition, serving, as her master did, with great distinction.

"Topsy" weathered the campaign practically from start to finish, although wounded at Guillaucourt, August, 1918. She was returned to Canada, where she has been used by the General ever since, (as at time of first publication), thus having gained a place in the roll of Canada's war horses.

"Dick."

"Dick" was the brown charger of Major-General W. A. Griesbach, C.B., C.M.G., D.S.O. His early life was spent in a racing stable at Edmonton, Alberta. He was never quite fast enough to win a race; his contribution to the work of the stable was rather that of a pace-maker.

In November, 1914. the Third Canadian Mounted Rifles were being organized at Edmonton, Alberta, and "Dick" was brought into that unit by Lieutenant E. G. Kendall. Shortly af-

"TOPSY"
The Charger of Brigadier-General A. H. Bell,
C.M.G., D.S.O.

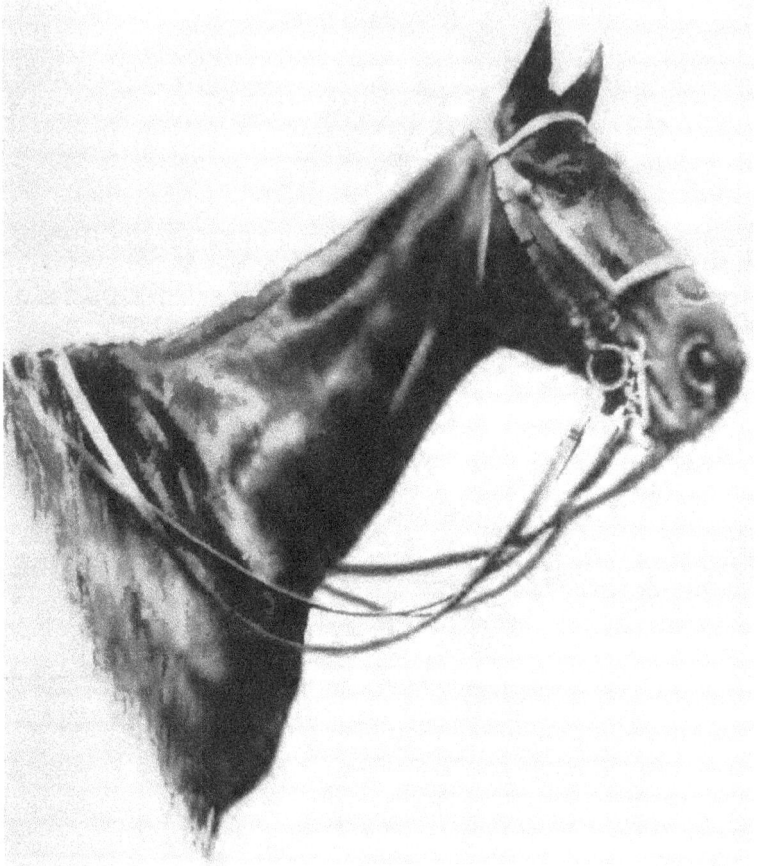

"DICK"
The Charger of Major-General W. A. Griesbach,
C.B., C.M.G., D.S.O.

ter this unit's arrival in France an order was issued to dismount same, and "Dick" fell into the hands of General Griesbach, who rode him continuously until the end of the war.

General Griesbach tried to ride "Dick" during the Battle of Vimy Ridge, but found that there was too much wire. He rode him on August 8, 1918, and on the 9th, and thereafter in all the actions that took place.

On the 2nd September, at Le Canal Du Nord, "Dick" was wounded and his groom killed. The general states:

'Dick' was a very nervous and sensitive horse; he knew perfectly well when he was in danger and seemed to associate dead men with danger, for at the sight of a dead or wounded man he always shied violently and had to be forced forward.

When 'Dick' was in bad humour he was very bad-tempered. In Germany, he walked across the yard one day and kicked a perfectly innocent man, and on another occasion I saw him bite a dog with no particular excuse or reason. He had a sort of melancholy disposition, and never seemed to get much pleasure out of life—quite unlike my second horse, 'Marie,' who enjoyed every moment.

I remember "Dick" when serving in the famous Forty-ninth Infantry Battalion; he was a well-known horse, but not so well-known as his gallant and distinguished master, who took a great pride in his horse.

"Dick" was returned to Canada and was stabled with the Lord Strathcona's Horse (R.C.) at Calgary, Alberta, doing his duty up until August 2, 1923, when it was my painful duty to destroy him on account of a compound fracture. He died while still serving King and country—a noble end for a noble creature.

"ABELLE GIRL."

"Abelle Girl," a light chestnut mare, was the charger of Colonel Sutherland Brown, C.M.G., D.S.O., First Canadian Division. Like most chargers, "Abelle Girl" was as well-known as her master, who rode her continually during the Great War. Although seldom nervous under shell fire, she had many narrow escapes, but came through the war without injury.

Colonel Brown rode "Abelle Girl" across the Rhine directly after Armistice, with the First Division. Upon demobilization this charger was returned to Canada, where she now enjoys a life of freedom, (as at time of first publication), in compensation for her faithful services to her master and country.

"Billy."

"Billy," the charger of Colonel W. W. P. Gibsone, C.M.G., C.B.E., D.S.O., was a bay gelding. The early history of this animal is rather obscure; I remember him well when with Headquarters Third Canadian Division. He was of a heavy type of saddle horse, and most suitable to carry the colonel, who was not a slim man by any means.

"Billy," like his master, was of a congenial turn of mind, and a great favourite; in short, nothing seemed to trouble him; the more work the merrier he seemed to be; scarcely a day sick.

I remember one occasion when he and his master came to grief at an inspection of one of the field ambulances in Mons. The colonel, riding with the G.O.C., came down the *boulevard* at a fairly good clip. On arrival at about the middle of the parade, the commanding officer yelled "Parade Attention," when the G.O.C.'s horse slipped and fell, rolling the general in the mud. "Billy," thinking, no doubt, that this was the correct thing to do, followed suit, and precipitated the colonel into the mud, much to his master's disgust, but to the amusement of those on parade, who considered the incident a terrible come-down, in more ways than one, for the G.O.C. and his Staff. Many, no doubt, were reminded of their own experiences in the Riding School, when, after being thrown from their mount, they heard the voice of the Riding Instructor shouting, "Who told you to dismount?"

"White Heather."

The charger of Colonel G. S. Cantlie, D.S.O., Forty-second Battalion, Montreal, was a perfect specimen of the equine race,

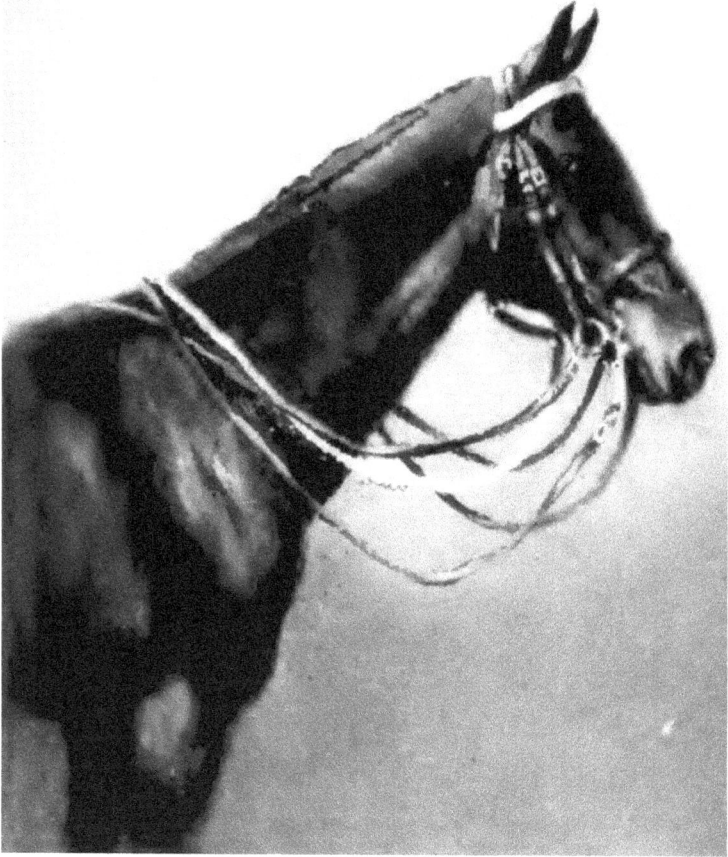

"ABELLE GIRL"
Charger of Colonel J. S. Brown, C.M.G., D.S.O.

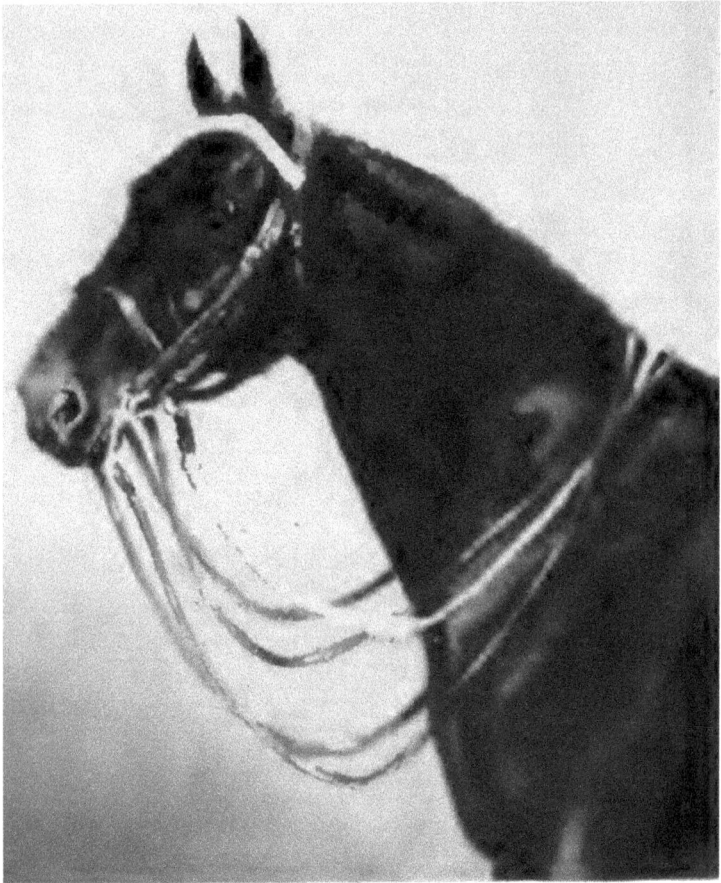

"Billy"
Charger of Colonel W. W. P. Gibsone,
C.M.G., C.B.E., D.S.O.

and was born on Alberta ranges.

"White Heather" commenced his career at the Quebec Tercentenary Celebration as an officer's charger in the R.N.W.M.P.

Later he was obtained by Colonel Cantlie and was taken overseas by that officer with the famous Forty-second Battalion from Montreal in June, 1915, and served with that regiment until returned to Canada after the war.

"White Heather" won many ribbons in France, and even after his return he followed the hounds of the Montreal Hunt Club for three seasons. He died in 1923 while pasturing in his master's estate at Point Claire, having fulfilled his duty to both master and country.

Colonel Cantlie's own words regarding his steed are as follows: "It is hard to part with 'White Heather.' but we gave him all the honours that could be bestowed upon a friend and a noble war horse."

"PETER."

"Peter," the charger of Colonel H. E. Snell, C.M.G., D.S.O., R.C.A.M.C, was purchased by that officer in 1911.

"Peter" in a sense was not a recruit at the outbreak of the Great War, for he served at militia camps of Petawawa, Kingston and London, so one may term him an old soldier.

I remember him well in France as the outstanding figure of the equine population of the Third Divisional Headquarters. He was a typical hunter, and loved to jump. He was in colour a golden chestnut.

"Peter" was wounded by shrapnel at the second Battle of Ypres in the woods surrounding Brielew Chateau, but was soon back on duty. Colonel Snell states:

'Peter' was known as the big horse of the Third Division, and by big I mean also the best. His height was used to good purpose at Villiers au Bois when the roof of the lean-to under which the divisional horses were stabled caved in. 'Peter,' being the highest horse, of course bore the brunt and held the roof off the rest of the little fellows. While he kicked up a little fuss, his good common sense kept him from injuring himself or the other horses.

For a big horse Peter was very handy, answered to all aids, and ran straight as an arrow to a tent peg. Needless to say his master was not an expert tent-pegger, for a peg from the top of a seventeen hand horse is a long way off, and looks small; nevertheless, 'Peter' did his part and ran straight.

In short, 'Peter' was a very wise animal and all that he needed was to be able to express his thoughts, and I feel that he could have told us lots worth hearing from which we might have learned a good deal.

After the war "Peter" was disposed of in Brussels to a private family. I was driving through the great park of that city in June, 1919, and met "Peter" with his new mistress astride. I spoke to her, and she informed me that "Peter" was a perfect gentleman, and further, that no money could buy him. With these few expressions from the rider, I left, contented that "Peter" had established himself and that he had found a fitting home.

"Theo."

The charger of Lieut.-Colonel G. R. Pearkes, V.C, D.S.O., M.C., Officer Commanding the 116th Canadian Infantry Battalion, C.E.F.

"Theo" was a thoroughbred mare, very keen and accomplished a great deal of work. In fact, the animal for its size exhibited great stability and often outclassed horses of a larger type.

She had a terrible disregard for ladies, and I remember her on one occasion precipitating a young lady over her head, no doubt taking this means of expressing her dislike to the fair sex.

In short, she was bold and fearless like her master, who was not only a brilliant and gallant soldier, but also a lover and friend of animals, both in times of war and peace.

"Flossy."

"Flossy" was taken overseas by Major R. S. Timmis, D.S.O.,

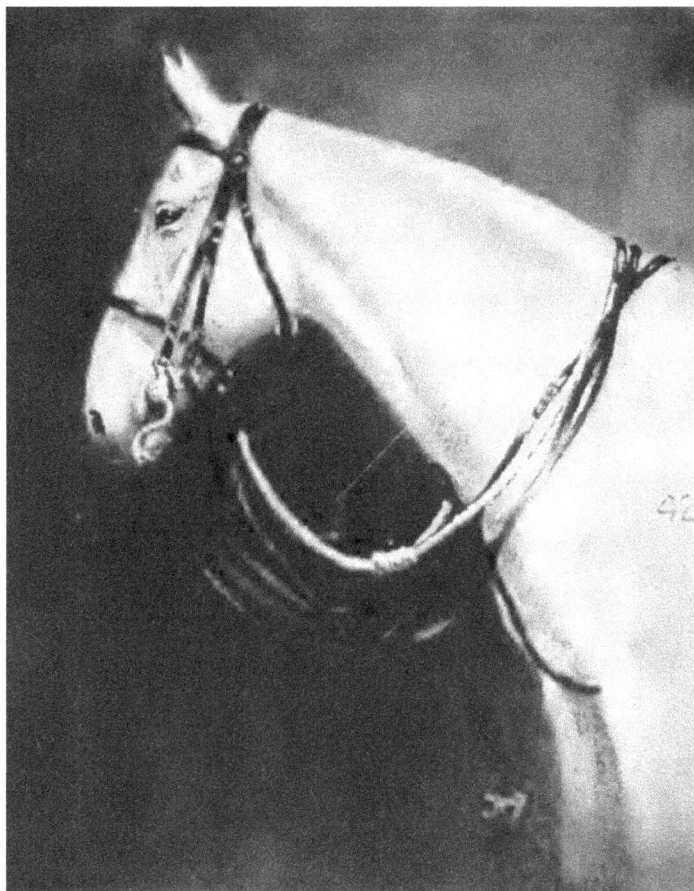

"WHITE HEATHER"
Charger of Lieut.-Colonel G. Cantlie, D.S.O.

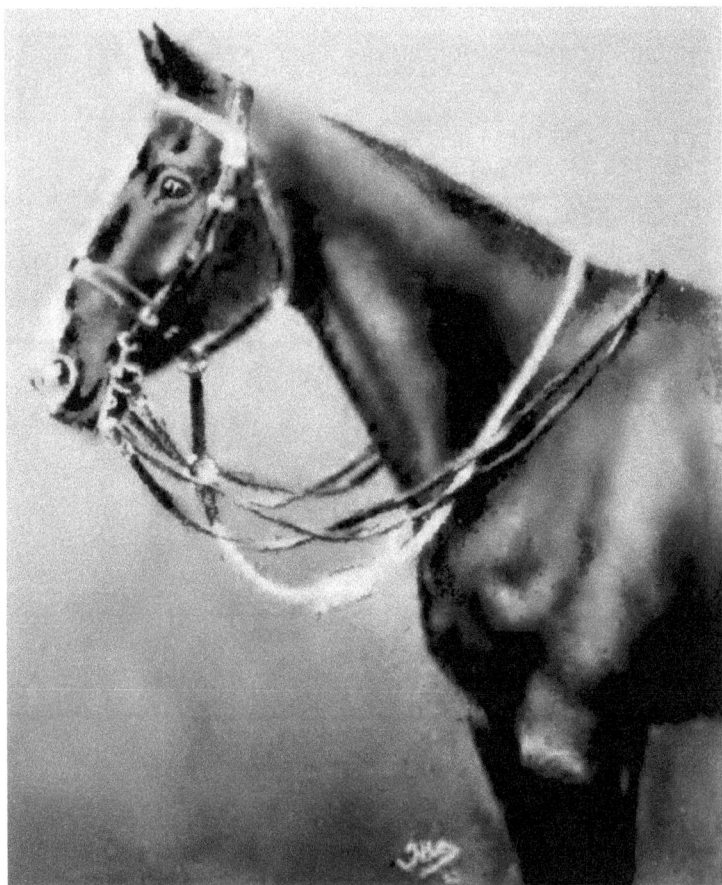

"PETER"
Charger of Colonel H. E. Snell, C.M.G., D.S.O.

"THEO"
The Charger of Lieut.-Colonel G. R. Pearkes,
V.C, D.S.O., M.C.

Royal Canadian Dragoons, a soldier of no mean distinction and a lover of horses.

Major Timmis purchased this animal from the Belgian Government after the Armistice, and returned it to Sir Fred Banbury's estate in Wiltshire, England, where it is now pensioned off with two other of his horses (as at time of first publication).

"Flossy" and her master were both severely wounded whilst reconnoitring near Achiet le Grand, on the Somme, during the month of July, 1916. Both, however, recovered very quickly and returned to duty.

"VIOLA."

The charger of Lieut.-Colonel T. C. Evans, M.C., A.D.V.S., 2nd Canadian Division.

"Viola" experienced long service in France, and was present at most of the important engagements, carrying her master on his many errands of mercy in tending to the wants of wounded and injured animals.

She was one of the outstanding horses of the 2nd Canadian Division, and for style there were few animals that could surpass her. The winner of many ribbons and admirers.

"Viola" was selected as one of the repatriated animals for return to Canada.

"BILLY POPE."

The charger of Lieutenant-Colonel P. J. Montague, C.M.G., D.S.O., M.C., was purchased in 1912, near Great Falls, Montana, as a six-year-old. He had been used for two years as a cow horse and was well trained in that work. He was brought to Winnipeg and used for polo only, in the seasons of 1912, 1913 and 1914; was mobilized in August, 1914, was put in the stables at Fort Osborne Barracks, and was shortly afterwards purchased by the Remount Commission.

He proceeded to England with the horses of the Sixth Canadian Infantry Brigade in May, 1915, crossed with his unit to France in September, 1915, and served continuously until Armistice, Nov. 11th, 1918. He was wounded, being hit by high

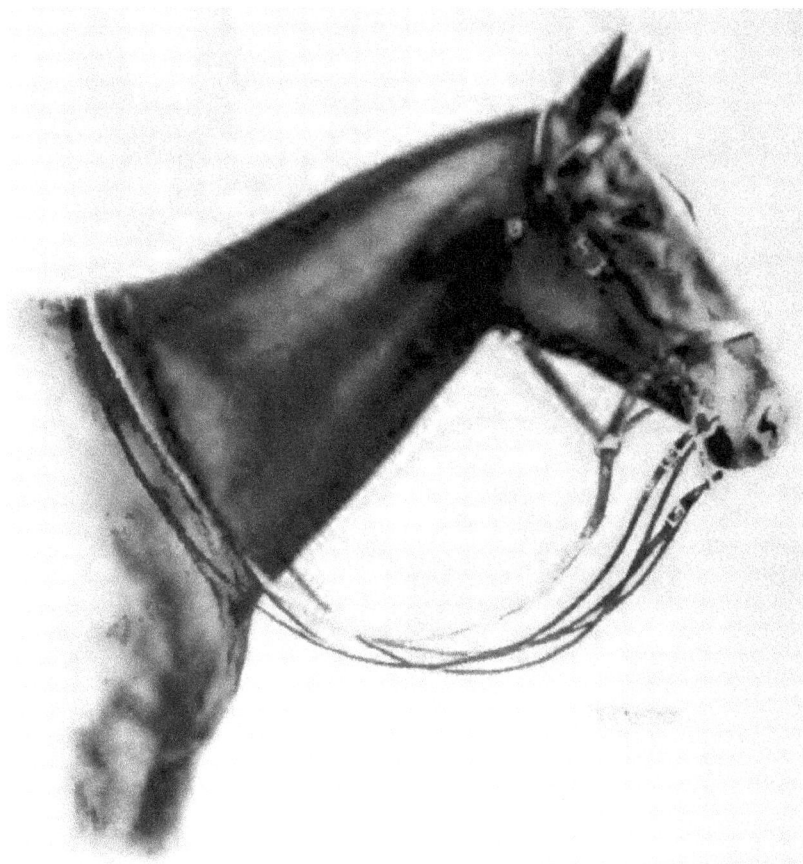

"FLOSSY"
Charger of Major R. Timmis, D.S.O.

"Viola"
Charger of Lieut.-Colonel T. C, Evans, M.C.

explosive shrapnel in the ribs, and apparently wounded in the lungs, while carrying his rider through the village of Wailly on the Arras front. He was evacuated through the excellent veterinary arrangements of the Second Canadian Division, to a Veterinary Aid Post, thence to the well-known low-slung horse ambulance of the Mobile Veterinary Section, and thence by empty supply train to the Veterinary General Hospital at Abbeville, where he remained until the middle of July.

While there he was operated on twice following X-ray work; incidentally this was during the time the Germans were bombing Abbeville, and his groom who had accompanied him found it necessary to lead him out at nights over a mile from the hospital. This went on for a period of six weeks, and shows the affection which men in the Expeditionary Force had for the animals they were looking after.

He was returned to duty just before the division proceeded to Amiens show, and marched with it in the ensuing operations, and afterwards to the Rhine, which he crossed with the division on the 13th December, 1918 He was one of the Canadian horses selected for repatriation, and on his way home was used for polo at Hurlingham during the summer. Since his return to Canada he has been used as a polo pony again during the seasons of 1921, 1922 and 1923, and has recently taken part in a tournament between the Winnipeg Clubs and the officers of the American army at Fort Snelling, Minnesota. During the polo season he is, of course, kept in Winnipeg, but during the rest of the year he is wintered on a farm near Lake Manitoba (as at time of first publication).

This animal has a wonderful memory, and the following story is related of him: In September, 1915, "Billy Pope" was billeted in the village of St. Marie Cappel, back of Bailleul; he was picketed in a yard behind the house on Main Street for a total of four days, and was not near this village again until the Division marched through it on the return from the Passchendaele operations in November, 1917. On that occasion he walked through the village alone with a slack rein, and on coming opposite the

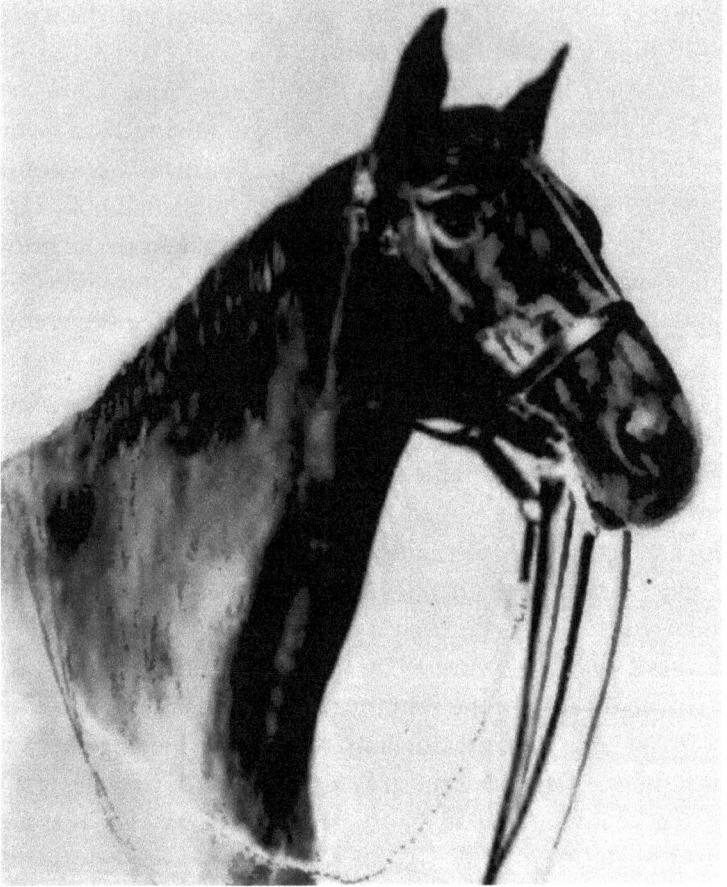

"BILLY POPE"
Charger of Lieut.-Colonel P. J. Montague,
C.M.G., D.S.O., M.C.

house where he had formerly been billeted he turned in and endeavoured to go through to the back.

In short, "Billy Pope," like his master, excelled himself in true British spirit, both in war and in peace.

"SNOOKUMS."

'Snookums," a chestnut gelding, the charger of Lieutenant-Colonel D. S. Tamblyn, D.S.O., O.B.E., was bred by W. D. McLennan, of Airdrie, Alberta, and proceeded overseas with the First Canadian Mounted Rifles.

This horse did an average of twenty miles a day for two years, and was wounded three times, twice at Ypres and the third time at Albert during the Canadian operations at these points. He, however, continued in service until the Armistice, and was disposed of to the Belgian Government, ultimately finding a home in Brussels, and was last seen carrying a gentleman through the famous park of that city.

"SANDY" AND "ZIZZI."

The chargers of Lieut.-Colonel A. Hamilton Gault, D.S.O., P.P.C.L.L

These animals proceeded overseas with their famous master and his regiment, and served through the war with distinction.

The pictures depict the animals at pasture in an Old Country park near Taunton, Somerset, England. The animals have been pensioned by Colonel A. Hamilton Gault for their long and faithful service to country and master.

Like the colonel, they were ever ready for the fray; no horses stood the terrible experiences of the Great War better than "Sandy" and "Zizzi."

They now run the green pastures in the park of their master, who felt that their faithfulness to him must be rewarded (as at time of first publication). This kindness to his dumb friends is but characteristic of Colonel A. Hamilton Gault and will give the reader some insight into the manner in which man appreciates the horse that has served him faithfully and well.

"SNOOKUMS"
Charger of Lieut.-Colonel D. S. Tamblyn, D.S.O., O.B.E.

"Star," the charger of Lieut.-Colonel R. C. Andros, D.S.O., Commanding 1st M. M. R.'s, was a pure Western animal, with quite a lot of blue blood running in his veins. He accompanied the regiment to France early in the war, and remained with that unit until after the entry into Mons, on Nov. 11, 1918. He died the following month after long and faithful service.

In the early part of "Star's" life he was considered an "outlaw," but was taken in hand by his master, who was a remarkable horseman, and by great kindness and patience became amenable to reason; in fact, quite a pet with the regiment, so much so that the colonel would turn him loose to graze while on the line of march, when, after satisfying his hunger, he would run along and take his place again in the ranks, following the bass drummer.

I remember both "Star" and his master well; they both exhibited that western spirit, especially the colonel. When an officer or man neglected an animal he had little respect for rank; when he found those who could not speak for themselves wanting or being abused, he would take such action as would be remembered for all future occasions. He was a lover of all animals and a friend to those who realized that their dumb charges depended upon them in regard to their wants and care. He preferred that a man should feed and water his horse before looking after his own requirements—a wonderful trait and an example for all to profit by.

"SANDY" AND "ZIZI" AFTER FOUR YEARS IN FRANCE
The Chargers of Lieut.-Colonel A. Hamilton Gault,
D.S.O., Commanding P.P.C.L.I.

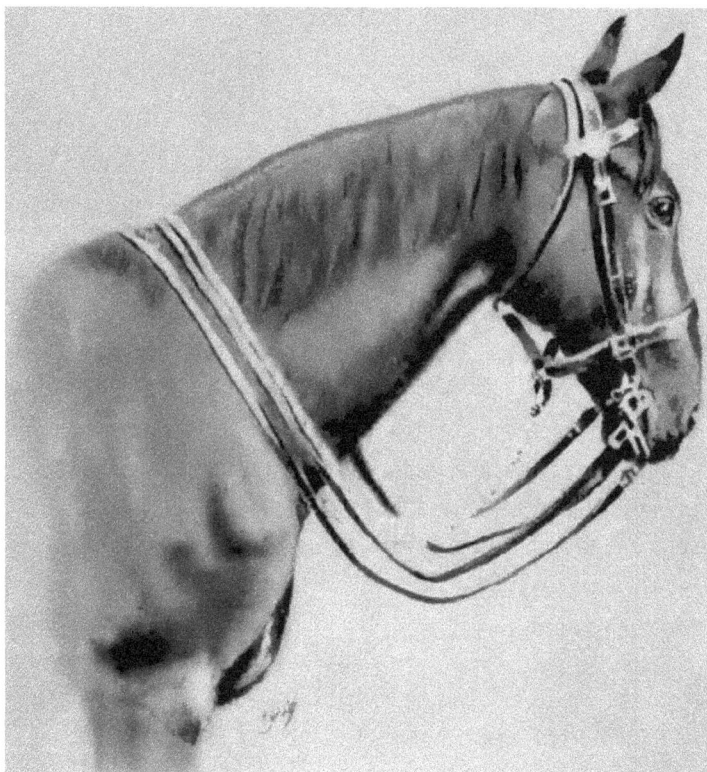

"STAR"
The Charger of Lieut.-Colonel R. C. Andros,
D.S.O., Commanding 1st C.M.R.'s.

CHAPTER 9

Dogs

It would not be fair if I did not refer to the canine race in this book and depict a few instances of its sagacity under war conditions.

During the conflict of nations man called his most useful servant, the horse, to assist him in his grim work of destruction, but he also took the dog into his confidence, because this animal was conscientious in the performance of its duty. Dogs were used as messengers and sentries in Red Cross work, telephone service, and in the transport of machine guns.

It was found by experience that the best breeds for ambulance work were Airedale terriers and German sheepdogs.

It was absolutely essential that ambulance dogs should be extremely wiry, hardy, and capable of great endurance, otherwise they were of little use. The manner in which these ambulance dogs were employed was to help the Red Cross men and doctors to search for wounded within a given area on a battlefield.

A dog's sense of scent and his acute hearing enabled him frequently to detect the breathing of a wounded man when a human ear could not detect it. Moreover, a puff of wind often sufficed to bring to a dog the scent of a man lying somewhere quite concealed.

These dogs were trained either to stay by a wounded man and to bark until the ambulance arrived, or to return at top speed to the ambulance, and then show those in charge the way to the wounded man.

GIVING A DOG A MESSAGE TO DELIVER

Ambulance dogs did not wear collars, for the wearing of such would have prevented them from getting through thickets and hedges impassable to man.

It has even happened that wounded men have been discovered lying under some hedge, or in some other spot where a human being would scarcely have discovered them, and it was in such cases as these that the ambulance dog proved especially useful.

The sentry dogs are most useful on outpost duty at night, however; their value consists in the fact that they can and do detect the approach of human beings some considerable time before the eye and the ear of the average person can distinguish anything. The result is that the sentry and patrol are fully on the alert, and it is impossible for them to be either ambushed or rushed. These dogs are never allowed to run loose, and no one is allowed to feed them except the man in charge of them. I should add that their method of indicating the approach of anyone at night is quite silent. It consists of a low growl and a stiffening of the body almost like a pointer.

Yet another use of dogs in warfare is that of spies. Part of the German system of espionage consisted in the employment of dogs which sometimes accompanied spies and returned to the German lines bearing messages. They were often sent out alone when a German force who did not know exactly where the line of attacking forces had been placed, was about to attack. The dogs were trained to run up to the Allies' line, and then to start barking loudly. For some time the English and French soldiers thought they were lost and gave them food, and tried to make pets of them; it was soon seen, however, that a German attack followed almost invariably on their arrival, and the order was regretfully given that any dogs which approached the outposts were to be shot.

Many of the dog anecdotes are full of pathos. It is recorded that in a field near Champguyon, the French soldiers were interred side by side in one grave, and the regimental dog, which refused to leave his dead comrades, kept guard over them.

A story is also related of a dog, a spaniel, which succeeded in finding his master, a soldier of a regiment which was engaged in the battle of the Marne. During the heavy fighting, the dog never left his master's side; immediately he saw his master fall he ran for the ambulance. When the ambulance men at Neaux realized that something was wrong, they followed the faithful dog and picked up the soldier; the animal accompanied his master to the railway station. It would have been cruel to separate the two friends, and so the dog went with his master to the hospital, from which both were later discharged.

This is not the only case of a dog's sagacity being instrumental in securing assistance, for a French soldier, writing to his family in Le Mans, tells how in all probability his life was saved by the pet dog of the regiment. Struck by a fragment of shell in the arm, with a bullet in his jaw, and a sabre cut over the head, the wounded man was lying half covered by the corpses of his comrades, when he felt a light touch on his forehead. It was "Tom," the regimental dog. In spite of the pain, the soldier tried to lift himself up a little; he knew that the dog was trained to carry to the camp a wounded man's *kepi*, but he had lost his. The brave dog hesitated and the man said to him, "Run along, Tom, go and find my comrades; get on, find them."

Tom understood; he dashed away to the camp, ran about among the men, pulling at their capes and barking, and succeeded in drawing two ambulance men to the spot, where the wounded man was lying, with the result that he was evacuated to hospital, where he made a complete recovery.

Dogs have served with distinction with many British regiments. They played a prominent part in the siege of Mafeking; one belonging to the base commandant was wounded three times.

A rough Irish terrier accompanied the Protectorate regiment in its engagements, and a third amused itself running after the small maxim shells, barking loudly and trying to retrieve pieces.

A contemporary recalls the feats of the famous war-dog "Drummer," which was attached to the regiment of the North-

FOR TELEPHONE SERVICE
A trained Airedale carrying a field telephone instrument.

umberland Fusiliers. "Drummer" was with the men all through the Egyptian campaign, was present at the battle of Omdurman, and assisted at the pacification of Crete. He also saw service at Gibraltar and in South Africa, where he went through the whole campaign with remarkable fortitude. He was present at Magersfontein, where Major Ray, son of his master, was killed. He was the only dog General Lord Methuen allowed to accompany his column from Orange River.

"Drummer" witnessed the relief of Kimberley, and Cecil Rhodes is reported to have given him a hearty meal to commemorate the event. He was wounded in the shoulder at Wynberg, and Her late Majesty Queen Victoria signified her intention of giving him a war medal on his return from South Africa. He had, however, miniature medals and clasps; the latter were for Diamond Hill, Johannesberg, Paardeburg, Driefontein, Relief of Kimberley, Belmont and Modder River.

Regimental Mascots and Pets

It is difficult to collect information regarding such animals as regimental mascots or pets after a war. However, I feel that these few anecdotes will serve the purpose of this book and give the reader an idea of the immense pleasure derived from such animals not only by units as a whole but by individuals.

The short account by Canon F. G. Scott, C.M.G., D.S.O., certainly depicts the inseparable feeling that exists, and describes the experiences which many men have met with, as also their love towards their dumb friends. His remark, "I loved you dearly, Dandy, and I wish I could pull down your soft face towards mine once again," is an expression no lover of animals can fail to comprehend.

The life history of "Sergt. Billy," the goat, 5th Canadian Infantry Battalion, by Lieut. E. N. Copping, is most interesting. A common remark in connection with this animal was that "Heine" couldn't get this unit's goat, and from what I know of the 5th Canadian Infantry Battalion Fritz did not.

The 8th Canadian Infantry Battalion took over with them

Camels taking a sea bath on the Palestine coast

a teddy bear mascot, but Teddy grew very large, so large that it was considered advisable to present him to the London Zoo in January of 1915. He is still there, (as at time of first publication), having grown to be a very fine animal and a great pet.

"Dandy"
Canon Scott's Pet Horse.
By Canon F. G. Scott, C.M.G., D.S.O.

When we were at Bethune a very important event in my military career took place. In answer to repeated requests, Head-quarters procured me a horse. I am told that the one sent to me came by mistake, and was not that which they intended me to have. The one I was to have, I heard, was the traditional pa-dre's horse, heavy, slow unemotional, and with knees ready at all times to sink in prayer. The animal sent to me, however, was a high-spirited chestnut thoroughbred, very pretty, very lively and neck-reined. It had once belonged to an Indian general, and was partly Arab.

Poor Dandy was my constant companion to the end. Dandy certainly was a beauty, and his lively disposition made him interesting to ride. I was able now to do much more parish visiting, and I was amused at the way in which my mount was inspected by the different grooms in our units. I had to stand the fire of much criticism. Evil and covetous eyes were cast upon Dandy. I was told he was "gone" in the knees. I was told he had a hump on the back—he was what is known as the "jumper's bump." Men tickled his back and, because he wriggled, told me he was "gone" in the kidneys.

I was told he was no proper horse for a *padre*, but that a fair exchange was always open to me. I was offered many an old transport hack for Dandy, and once was even asked if I would change him for a pair of mules. I took all the criticisms under consideration, and then when they were repeated I told the men that really I loved to ride a horse with a hump on its back. It was so biblical, just like riding a camel. As for bad kidneys, both Dandy and I were teetotallers, and we could arrest disease by our temperance habits. The weakness of knees too was no objection to my eyes. In fact, I had so long, as a parson, sat over weak-kneed congregations that I felt quite at home sitting on a weak-kneed horse.

EPITAPH.

Poor dear old Dandy, many were the rides we had together. Many were the jumps we took. Many were the ditches we tumbled into. Many were the unseen barbed wires and overhanging telephone wires which we broke, you with your chest and I with my nose and forehead. Many were the risks we ran in front of batteries in action which neither of us had observed till we found ourselves deafened with a hideous explosion and wrapped in flame. I loved you dearly, Dandy, and I wish I could pull down your soft face towards mine once again, and talk of the times you took me down Hill 63 and along Hyde Park Corner at Ploegsteert.

Had I not been wounded and sent back to England at the end of the war, I would have brought you home with me to show to my family, a friend that not merely uncomplainingly but cheerfully, with prancing feet and arching neck and well-groomed skin, bore me safely through dangers and darkness, on crowded roads and untracked fields. What dances we have had together. Dandy, when I have got the bands to play a waltz and you have gone through the twists and turns of a performance in which you took an evident delight. I used to tell the men that Dandy and I always came home together. Sometimes I was on his back and sometimes he was on mine, but we always came home together.

"PHILO"
Canon Scott's Pet Dog.
By Canon F. G. Scott, C.M.G., D.S.O.

A few days later, my establishment was increased by the purchase of a well-bred little white fox terrier. He rejoiced in the name of "Philo," and became my inseparable companion. The men called him my "Curate." Dandy, Philo and I made a family party which was bound together by very close ties of affection. Though none of us could speak the language of the others, yet the sympathy of each enabled us to understand and appreciate one another's opinions. I always knew what Dandy thought and what he would do. I always knew too what Philo was thinking about.

Philo had a great horror of shells. I put this down to the fact that he was born at Beuvry, a place which had been long under shell-fire. When he heard a shell coming in his direction, Philo used to go to the door of the dugout and listen for the explosion, and then come back to me in a state of whining terror. He could not even stand the sound of our own guns. It made him run round and round barking and howling furiously.

"SERGEANT BILLY"
By E. N. Copping,
Ex-Lieutenant 5th Canadian Infantry Battalion.

Billy was a goat, but no ordinary goat, mark you, for he wore upon his tawny, unkempt back a scarlet jacket emblazoned with the colours of the 5th Canadian Infantry, the chevrons of a sergeant, stripes for wounds received and for services rendered, together with the ribbons of the Mons Star, the General Service, and the rainbow-coloured riband of the Victory Medal.

In August, 1914, Billy was leading a peaceful goat-like existence at Broadview, Saskatchewan, until one Sunday morning his little mistress presented him to a train-load of Western troopers, upon whose car was scrolled in white chalk lettering, "Berlin or Bust." He was adopted by this motley crowd and taken by them, first to Valcartier Camp, and then across the seas to another training camp in England.

After months of training, word came for the battalion to proceed to the front, but orders were issued that no regimental pets were to be taken into France. Great was the consternation at the thought of leaving behind Billy. "We can get another colonel," cried the boys, "but not another goat." At night Billy was concealed in a wagon, covered with a tarpaulin, and smuggled on to the transport, and from it off and on to the troop train. And when the regiment disembarked at a little Flemish station and marched away up the white-cobbled road, Billy was with it, bringing up the rear with the transport section.

His career in France was not at first a happy one, and he was even suspected of being a spy. On one occasion he was discovered by the battalion sergeant-major devouring the Nominal Roll. An attempt by this important personage to rescue the manuscript resulted in his sacred person getting butted out of the tent.

But in time Billy lived down this evil reputation. During the confusion and shambles of the second battle of Ypres, he was discovered in a shell crater bleeding from a shrapnel wound and, so his rescuers report, standing guard over a wounded and much terrified Prussian Guardsman.

A year later Billy was again wounded. He recovered, always to limp, was promoted to sergeant, and relegated to a job behind the lines. He always joined the regiment on parade, however, bedizened in his scarlet coat, and with golden tassels on his horns.

Finally, after four and a half years of service, he returned from the war and marched in triumph at the head of his battalion through the streets of his home town. He was returned to his former mistress, who endeavoured to re-establish him in the ways of peace.

But it was too tame an existence for Billy. He pined for the old devil-may-care days of the campaign and for his old comrades-in-arms, and in so doing faded and died.

His skin has been preserved, stuffed and mounted, and placed in the G.W.V.A. Headquarters in Regina, Sask., later to be removed to the Provincial Museum. And there he stands with his shaggy beard and twisted horns, arrayed in all his trappings as an example to all goats—AND TO MANY MEN.

8TH CANADIAN INFANTRY BATTALION'S TEDDY BEAR.

An interesting story was related to me by the officer who

was more or less responsible for this animal, regarding a little incident which took place in London prior to the battalion proceeding to France.

Meeting a pal who was anxious to play a practical joke, it was arranged to give a dinner to some friends at one of the leading hotels. All was set for the party, and the officer in charge of the bear proceeded to the zoo, procured Teddy and brought him down to the hotel in a taxi and ushered him into a small room adjoining the private dining-room in which the dinner was being held, while the only other exit from the dining-room was secured, and at a given signal Teddy was turned loose into the dining-room, to the consternation and demoralization of all present.

Tables were overturned, plates and dishes were deposited on the floor, and frantic attempts were made to get away by all, while Teddy sat just inside the door growling and adding to the excitement.

Some held chairs on high to strike in event of an attack from the intruder, while others were between two frames of mind, whether to jump out of the window or fight it out on the dining-room floor. Suddenly my friend opened the door of the dining-room and apologized and enquired whether they had seen a bear, and, much to the disgust of those present, Teddy went to his master, and was borne away to the great relief of all, who sank into their chairs and partook of stimulants to brace themselves up after the ordeal, while my friend experienced a terrible time in getting Teddy back to the zoo, his home of the future.

I understand he made numerous attempts to get away, and even got the taxi driver's nerve, for he had not bargained to drive such a woolly customer through the streets of London. However, everything ended happily, while those present certainly will never forget the evening spent with Teddy.

DUMB HEROES.

There's a D.S.O. for the Colonel,
A Military Cross for the Sub,
A medal or two when we all get through,
And a bottle of wine with our grub.

There's a stripe of gold for the wounded,
A rest by the bright sea-shore,
And a service is read when we bury our dear,
Then the country has one hero more.

But what of our poor dumb heroes,
They are sent without choice to the fight,
That strain at the load, on the shell-swept road,
As they take up the rations at night.

They are shelling on Hellfire Corner,
Their shrapnel fast burst on the Square,
And the bullets drum, as the transports come.
With the food for the soldiers there.

The halt till the shelling is over.
The rush through the lines of fire.
The glaring light, in the dead of night.
And the terrible sight in the mire.

It's the daily work of the heroes.
And they answer the spur and rein,
With quickened breath, 'mid the toll of death.
In the mud and holes and the rain.

There's a fresh healed wound in the chestnut.
The black mare's neck has a mark;
The brown mule's new mate won't keep the same gait
As the one killed last night in the dark.

But they walk with the spirit of heroes,
They dare, not for medals or cross.
But for duty alone, into perils unknown.
They go, never counting their loss.

There's a swift painless death for the hopeless,

130

With a grave in a shell-hole or field,
There's a hospital base for the casualty case,
And a vet for those easily healed.

But there's never a shadow of glory,
A cheer or a speech in their praise,
As patient and true they carry us through.
With the limbers on shot-riven ways.

So here's to dumb heroes of Britain,
Who serve her so nobly and true,
As the best of her sons, 'mid the roar of the guns.
And the best of her boys on the blue.

They are shell-shocked, they're bruised and they're broken,
They are wounded and torn as they fall.
But they are true and they're brave, to the very grave,
And they're heroes—one and all.

        —Captain T. Girling.

A TIMELY DRINK

LEONAUR

ALSO FROM LEONAUR
AVAILABLE IN SOFTCOVER OR HARDCOVER WITH DUST JACKET

WINGED WARFARE *by William A. Bishop*—The Experiences of a Canadian 'Ace' of the R.F.C. During the First World War.

THE STORY OF THE LAFAYETTE ESCADRILLE *by George Thenault*—A famous fighter squadron in the First World War by its commander..

R.F.C.H.Q. *by Maurice Baring*—The command & organisation of the British Air Force during the First World War in Europe.

SIXTY SQUADRON R.A.F. *by A. J. L. Scott*—On the Western Front During the First World War.

THE STRUGGLE IN THE AIR *by Charles C. Turner*—The Air War Over Europe During the First World War.

WITH THE FLYING SQUADRON *by H. Rosher*—Letters of a Pilot of the Royal Naval Air Service During the First World War.

OVER THE WEST FRONT *by "Spin" & "Contact"* —Two Accounts of British Pilots During the First World War in Europe, Short Flights With the Cloud Cavalry by "Spin" and Cavalry of the Clouds by "Contact".

SKYFIGHTERS OF FRANCE *by Henry Farré*—An account of the French War in the Air during the First World War.

THE HIGH ACES *by Laurence la Tourette Driggs*—French, American, British, Italian & Belgian pilots of the First World War 1914-18.

PLANE TALES OF THE SKIES *by Wilfred Theodore Blake*—The experiences of pilots over the Western Front during the Great War.

IN THE CLOUDS ABOVE BAGHDAD *by J. E. Tennant*—Recollections of the R. F. C. in Mesopotamia during the First World War against the Turks.

THE SPIDER WEB *by P. I. X. (Theodore Douglas Hallam)*—Royal Navy Air Service Flying Boat Operations During the First World War by a Flight Commander

ACCOUNTS OF THE WRECK OF THE COMMERCE *by James Riley & Archibald Robbins*—Two Narratives of Shipwreck, Capture and Slavery by Arabs of American Seamen, 1815. *An Authentic Narrative of the Loss of the American Brig "Commerce"* by James Riley and *A Journal Comprising an Account of the Loss of the Brig "Commerce", of Hartford, (Con.) James Riley, Master* by Archibald Robbins.

AVAILABLE ONLINE AT **www.leonaur.com**
AND FROM ALL GOOD BOOK STORES
07/09

LEONAUR

ALSO FROM LEONAUR
AVAILABLE IN SOFTCOVER OR HARDCOVER WITH DUST JACKET

A HISTORY OF THE 17TH AERO SQUADRON *by Frederick Mortimer Clapp*—An American Squadron on the Western Front During the First World War.

RICHTHOFEN & BOELCKE IN THEIR OWN WORDS *by Manfred Freiher von Richthofen & Oswald Böelcke*—The Red Battle Flyer by Manfred Freiher von Richthofen and An Aviator's Field Book by Oswald Böelcke.

WITH THE FRENCH FLYING CORPS *by Carroll Dana Winslow*—The Experiences of an American Pilot During the First World War.

EN L'AIR *by Bert Hall*—The Experiences of an American Foreign Legionnaire as a Pilot With the Lafayette Escadrille on the Western Front and in the East During the First World War.

"AMBULANCE 464" ENCORE DES BLESSÉS *by Julien H. Bryan*—The experiences of an American Volunteer with the French Army during the First World War

THE GREAT WAR IN THE MIDDLE EAST: 1 *by W. T. Massey*—The Desert Campaigns & How Jerusalem Was Won---two classic accounts in one volume.

THE GREAT WAR IN THE MIDDLE EAST: 2 *by W. T. Massey*—Allenby's Final Triumph.

SMITH-DORRIEN *by Horace Smith-Dorrien*—Isandlwhana to the Great War.

1914 *by Sir John French*—The Early Campaigns of the Great War by the British Commander.

GRENADIER *by E. R. M. Fryer*—The Recollections of an Officer of the Grenadier Guards throughout the Great War on the Western Front.

BATTLE, CAPTURE & ESCAPE *by George Pearson*—The Experiences of a Canadian Light Infantryman During the Great War.

HEAVY FIGHTING BEFORE US *by George Brenton Laurie*—The Letters of an Officer of the Royal Irish Rifles on the Western Front During the Great War.

THE CAMELIERS *by Oliver Hogue*—A Classic Account of the Australians of the Imperial Camel Corps During the First World War in the Middle East.

RED DUST *by Donald Black*—A Classic Account of Australian Light Horsemen in Palestine During the First World War.

AVAILABLE ONLINE AT **www.leonaur.com**
AND FROM ALL GOOD BOOK STORES

07/09

LEONAUR

ALSO FROM LEONAUR
AVAILABLE IN SOFTCOVER OR HARDCOVER WITH DUST JACKET

FARAWAY CAMPAIGN *by F. James*—Experiences of an Indian Army Cavalry Officer in Persia & Russia During the Great War.

REVOLT IN THE DESERT *by T. E. Lawrence*—An account of the experiences of one remarkable British officer's war from his own perspective.

MACHINE-GUN SQUADRON *by A. M. G.*—The 20th Machine Gunners from British Yeomanry Regiments in the Middle East Campaign of the First World War.

A GUNNER'S CRUSADE *by Antony Bluett*—The Campaign in the Desert, Palestine & Syria as Experienced by the Honourable Artillery Company During the Great War .

DESPATCH RIDER *by W. H. L. Watson*—The Experiences of a British Army Motorcycle Despatch Rider During the Opening Battles of the Great War in Europe.

TIGERS ALONG THE TIGRIS *by E. J. Thompson*—The Leicestershire Regiment in Mesopotamia During the First World War.

HEARTS & DRAGONS *by Charles R. M. F. Crutwell*—The 4th Royal Berkshire Regiment in France and Italy During the Great War, 1914-1918.

INFANTRY BRIGADE: 1914 *by John Ward*—The Diary of a Commander of the 15th Infantry Brigade, 5th Division, British Army, During the Retreat from Mons.

DOING OUR 'BIT' *by Ian Hay*—Two Classic Accounts of the Men of Kitchener's 'New Army' During the Great War including *The First 100,000* & *All In It*.

AN EYE IN THE STORM *by Arthur Ruhl*—An American War Correspondent's Experiences of the First World War from the Western Front to Gallipoli-and Beyond.

STAND & FALL *by Joe Cassells*—With the Middlesex Regiment Against the Bolsheviks 1918-19.

RIFLEMAN MACGILL'S WAR *by Patrick MacGill*—A Soldier of the London Irish During the Great War in Europe including *The Amateur Army*, *The Red Horizon* & *The Great Push*.

WITH THE GUNS *by C. A. Rose & Hugh Dalton*—Two First Hand Accounts of British Gunners at War in Europe During World War 1- Three Years in France with the Guns and With the British Guns in Italy.

THE BUSH WAR DOCTOR *by Robert V. Dolbey*—The Experiences of a British Army Doctor During the East African Campaign of the First World War.

AVAILABLE ONLINE AT www.leonaur.com
AND FROM ALL GOOD BOOK STORES

07/09

www.ingramcontent.com/pod-product-compliance
Lightning Source LLC
Chambersburg PA
CBHW031855090426
42741CB00005B/506

9780857067869